ADRIAN MCNALLY SMITH

A RELUCTANT SEARCH FOR SPIRITUAL TRUTHS

ADRIAN MCNALLY SMITH

A RELUCTANT SEARCH FOR SPIRITUAL TRUTHS

THE ACORN PRESS
CHARLOTTETOWN
2020

AC⬡RNPRESS

P.O. Box 22024
Charlottetown, Prince Edward Island
C1A 9J2
acornpresscanada.com

Printed in Canada
Edited by Penelope Jackson
Copy edit by Laurie Brinklow
Designed by Matt Reid

Library and Archives Canada Cataloguing in Publication

Title: A reluctant search for spiritual truths / Adrian McNally Smith.
Names: Smith, Adrian McNally, 1961- author.
Description: Includes bibliographical references.
Identifiers: Canadiana (print) 20200218565 | Canadiana (ebook) 20200218573 |
ISBN 9781773660493 (softcover) | ISBN 9781773660554 (HTML)
Subjects: LCSH: Smith, Adrian McNally, 1961-—Religion. |
LCSH: Spiritual biography. | LCSH: Spirituality. |
LCSH: Forgiveness—Religious aspects. | LCGFT: Autobiographies.
Classification: LCC BL73.S65 A3 2020 | DDC 204.092—dc23

The publisher acknowledges the support of the Government of Canada
through the Canada Book Fund of the Department of Canadian
Heritage and the Canada Council for the Arts Block Grant Program.

For Willow, Poppy, and Jane

There are only two ways to live your life.
One is as though nothing is a miracle.
The other is as though everything is a miracle.

-Attributed to Albert Einstein

Spirituality is an awareness that there is something far
greater than we are, something that created this universe,
created life, and that we are an authentic, important,
significant part of it, and can contribute to its evolution.

-Elisabeth Kübler-Ross

We are not human beings having a spiritual experience.
We are spiritual beings having a human experience.

-Pierre Teilhard de Chardin

Author's Note

WHEN I WROTE MY BOOK *Finding Forgiveness* about my ever-evolving relationship with my father, a few close friends read my initial draft. My good friend Alan Edwards was honest and open with me. He said, "Adrian, you have two books here in one," and he suggested that I separate the two themes; namely, the psychological process of reaching forgiveness and, secondly, the role that spirituality played in my life. While the two themes were deeply interwoven, they were also separate entities.

My wife, Cheryl, agreed with Alan. Cheryl suggested that I complete my writing about my father, believing that that was the most pressing issue at hand, for I had been dealing with that matter for a very long time. She explained that she did not believe my concept of spirituality was fully developed; she feared I was not ready to tackle that more mystical subject. Both my friend and my wife were correct.

Then another reader and close friend, Glenn Edison, offered a unique perspective. Glenn argued that in my initial drafts of *Finding Forgiveness* I was intentionally minimizing what constituted the "spiritual events" in my life so as to not take away from the story of forgiveness. He proposed that I was not doing the topic of spirituality justice. To further complicate the situation, Glenn knew that I had assumed everyone had similar spiritual experiences to my own, a point which he adamantly disagreed with. As direct as Glenn could be, he assured me that he hadn't experienced them, and he strongly encouraged me to be more open, to find that voice, to take that risk.

So here I am today.

In *Finding Forgiveness*, I deliberately did not emphasize my spiritual experiences, for my focus in that writing was on the importance of change and transformation. I dwelled on the struggles I had endured and the process I underwent when I discovered my father's past, as I moved from the stages of denial, anger, and depression towards acceptance and eventually forgiveness. I dwelled on the everyday aspects of my struggles that I felt people in general might be best able to relate to. I wanted people to know that change was possible and that, in the end, forgiveness was an ultimate source of peace and healing.

Finding Forgiveness holds much more detail about my family life, but, briefly, I discovered after my father's death first that he had been a closeted homosexual, and then that he had committed sexual abuse. When I learned of my father's hidden life as a homosexual man, I had already endured a few powerful, inexplicable spiritual experiences. These experiences would foster a level of trust that there was much more to life than the physical dimensions, which would help guide me through my struggles with my father's legacy. Though the initial path was long, I did endure, and life did get significantly better. And later, when allegations of sexual abuse surfaced against my father, this time I healed much more quickly, trusting even more deeply. The same rationale was applicable to my physical struggles. I had overcome significant challenges before, and my conviction did not falter. I believed that I would recover again. In both domains, physical and emotional, my spiritual beliefs were instrumental in my healing and recovery.

In writing *Finding Forgiveness*, I shared the truth of my family's dysfunction—the lies, the betrayal, the secrets—and the world didn't end. When I allowed myself to be completely vulnerable, I was actually overwhelmed by the emotional support I received and the number of people who shared how my story helped them on their personal journeys.

Truth causes change. Truth is never wrong.

That experience encouraged me to be equally open about the other truths in my life, particularly the spiritual truths of my life thus far. For I had to acknowledge that when I denied my spiritual experiences, I was, in fact, not accepting myself.

I have deliberately written this book from a personal perspective, sharing personal examples of spirit in my life, not because my life is more special or spiritual than anyone else's, but rather to show how anyone can experience spiritual truths if they remain open and willing to see their concept of God/Spirit in their everyday lives, for spirituality thrives in humanity—real life.

An ancient Buddhist teaching states that those people who are allowed to see the truth are obligated to communicate the truth to others, to share their knowledge with others. This was their bargain of knowing: a bodhisattva vow.

My bodhisattva vow is to share something far greater than we are, to show that there is more to this world than meets the eye, and to encourage the belief that we are an authentic and significant part of it and its evolution... to speak what feels unspeakable. So how do I know that this is my story to tell? Because I am scared to death of doing so.

This book, thereby, once again, is my bodhisattva vow, my bargain of knowing.

Prologue

WHEN I WAS EIGHT, Father caught a summer flu that stayed with him for days. It was rare for him to be sick. On the Sunday that fell within these days, because my mother did not drive, Father got out of bed and drove us all to church. Hayden, my brother, was an altar boy, so he got out of the car and scurried to the back entrance of St. Augustine's Roman Catholic Church. Father said he would wait in the car for a while to determine how he was feeling. Mother decided to head on in and join in the communal saying of the rosary. By now, my reluctance to attend church and my restlessness within church were well known. Surprisingly, Mother did not encourage me to come along with her that morning.

"Wait here with your father," Mother said, speaking over the back of the car seat, before she proceeded to get out and shut the car door.

"I'm not feeling so well," Father admitted after a few minutes of silence. "I'd best not chance it. Do you want to join your mother?"

It was a foolish question. I was an introvert who always felt most at home with nature rather than with crowds of people.

"I'll stay with you," I answered.

Father started the car and drove off past the stone arch entrance, past the idle tombstones that lined the rows of the dead, past the Belcourt Centre, where the nuns resided, and the two of us ended up at the shore—a strip of sandbar located at the end of a dirt road tucked well in back behind the church. The beach was isolated that Sunday morning, except for Father and me and an array of birds. I spent that glorious morning in the warm summer sun skipping rocks and collecting seashells, my father close at hand. I watched a flock of sandpipers scurrying along the water's edge, rushing out into the receding sea to pick at the washed-ashore morsels of food, only to quickly retreat when the tide came back in. My attention was briefly diverted to a flock of seagulls passing overhead, their wings flapping in unison, their voices calling out to one another. As I followed the path of their flight, I noticed the steeple of St. Augustine's Church that loomed off in the far distance. I felt closer to God/Spirit than at any other moment in my young life. I knew what I was experiencing wasn't an everyday occurrence.

It was as if time stood still.

Ironically, this experience had everything and nothing to do with religion.

On that beautiful sunny morning, while walking along the sandy north shore, surrounded by nature in the private company of my father, I had no idea at the time that I was experiencing an early awakening to what I would eventually come to know as a peak experience. I knew that what I felt was euphoric, that it was a moment of the highest happiness, that it felt perfect, and that I would always long to repeat the experience... as it felt beautiful, true, and real.

It was the knowing that a divine source operates through each and every one of us. And what you call this source—Spirit, Energy, Essence, Divine Intelligence, Consciousness, One, Allah, Goddess, or God—has little bearing. Nothing could matter less. That was my first spiritual truth: the source of creation is the same.

Standing there, feeling the sand beneath my feet, I continued to look at the steeple in the far-off distance, and I suddenly became aware that some people did find God in my childhood church— certainly they could, just as others could find God in any other church, mosque, or temple. Though I couldn't reason this at the time, I came to know that all major religions can serve a purpose in providing direction and guidance; each is but one of many means and paths, all with the identical goal of encouraging and fostering a relationship with your Creator.

I was only eight, but I was touched by the extraordinary of the ordinary. My God/Spirit was everywhere, especially in people and nature, as opposed to any religious institution.

Peak experiences can be a gateway to attaining spiritual awareness.

When American psychologist Abraham H. Maslow originally coined the term "peak experience," he was referring to those intense moments of joy and happiness that create states of harmony, interconnectedness, and revelation. He believed these experiences were often marked by their mystical or spiritual significance, as they often offered insight into the meaning and value of existence for those who endured them. He believed that individuals actually transcended ego during such experiences. Maslow proceeded to write that a person who might experience a peak experience eventually "discovers, develops, and retains his own religion"… that these peak experiences become part of "their personal therapy, personal growth, or personal fulfilment." In a later book, *Toward a Psychology of Being*, Maslow calls these experiences "life-validating."

I cannot put parameters around these experiences, but will say that, in my case, these experiences have generally happened to me when I am deeply concerned for those I love, in times when I am surrounded by nature and/or animals, in moments of quiet and solitude, or in times of deep thought. In my own life, these experiences have ranged from simple, unpretentious incidents to more life-altering events. For even in times of strife and misery, I have found wondrous moments of insight, but also atonement, stillness, and peace. I have found that these moments that occur in the middle of disarray are truly the most profound and meaningful, permanently affecting my approach to and my view of life. These moments of such intensity have allowed me to overcome many obstacles and have provided meaning when everything else around me seemed to fail. And regardless of the magnitude of the activity, I have always felt like I was in the presence of a higher power, and an inner feeling of complete, unwavering trust has always prevailed. Life has allowed me to look at the world through this spiritual lens.

In addition to peak experiences, this spiritual essence came into my life by developing my intuition, creating meaningful coincidences in my life, and intervening in my world in times of need. Some of the lessons I received were life changing; others were subtler, as in simple reminders or nudges, more ordinary. Often a thought or visualization will come to mind during meditation or while I am walking along the shore or in the sanctuary of the woods—these moments are very different from my conscious and normal ways of thinking. Sometimes the messages would come in my dreams. When I listened to my dreams and intuition, things seemed to fall into place. Some of the lessons were easily learned, while others took ages to be realized.

One of my initial challenges was that I wanted to differentiate the experiences, meaning that while some experiences felt mystical in nature, more at home in a religious or spiritual context, others fitted nicely into the realms of philosophy and psychology. Author Robert Wright helped bring a degree of clarity when he pointed out that many aspects of nirvana form "a kind of intersection between the exotically metaphysical and the naturalistic." He uses the practice of mindfulness meditation as an example. It can act as a bridge. Regardless if you are looking for a sense of peace and calmness in the present moment or are seeking enlightenment, it's the same essential tool. So why question?

So regardless of their intensity or brevity, all experiences were essential for my overall development. All were real, and all were reminders that there is a far greater energy to this world than meets the human eye. The universe was conspiring for my greatest good and that of those around me. It was insights and learning, and they were all messages of hope.

My sense of spirituality became a mosaic of many seemingly unconnected tiles. There were situations in life that challenged me to learn from them; to discover new levels of kindness, empathy, faithfulness, acceptance, and love; to develop patience, understanding, and mindfulness. And somehow, the intent was that through my learning, maybe someone else's life might also be made better—maybe even in ways that I would never comprehend or need to know—as my life was greatly enriched by the lives of others who entered mine.

These spiritual experiences were personal learning experiences that spoke directly to me, as everyone has his or her own particular lessons to learn in this life. And while I have remained nonreligious in the conventional sense, these spiritual experiences became the grounds of my relationship with my Creator. And I have spent my life privately welcoming the presence of this spiritual essence.

The first lesson I had to learn was intimate and personal: I had to accept that what I was experiencing was real and that I was not insane. I could not expect everyone else to share my beliefs, but I could choose not to live in fear of rejection or ridicule. Once I accepted my experiences as real, my intuition became stronger; life became easier and far more meaningful. And all along my journey, I was forever reminded that I had free will. At any point,

I could choose to deny my experiences; I could choose to return to a life of fear and conformity, or I could choose to learn from my experiences. The choice was mine. It was that simple. It was my responsibility and only my responsibility.

The second lesson, more comprehensive and inclusive, centred on self-actualization.

In the July 1943 edition of *Psychological Review*, A. H. Maslow wrote a paper entitled "A Theory of Human Motivation." Among the various propositions presented, Maslow claimed that all behaviour is motivated and that it is biological, culturally, and situationally determined. If our basic needs are met—namely, physiological, safety, love, and esteem—then we will experience the need to become everything that we are capable of becoming. He writes, "What a man can be, he must be." He referred to this need as self-actualization.

I gradually came to believe that everything in my life happened for a greater purpose, that of learning certain essential lessons in life and helping others.

So I asked myself, when is life most meaningful?

The answer: when there is love, and when I know there is something more.

PART I

Ye might be partakers of the divine nature.

2 Peter 1:4

Learn from yesterday, live for today, hope for tomorrow.
The important thing is not to stop questioning.

Attributed to Albert Einstein

THE FIRST TIME GOD SPOKE TO ME I was eight years old, and I was standing alone in the living room of my childhood home, looking out through my favourite window, gazing out upon nature. It was like time stood still.

On that spring morning in Oyster Bed Bridge, the experience was brief and an insight or knowledge was given; I felt as if I was under the influence of a higher power or some divine source of energy, so at that young age I could only call it God, for I knew of no other name. I knew this voice was completely trustworthy and was there to look after me.

The voice told me that the religious stories the church had taught me, reinforced by my parents and my Catholicism classes, were not true.

Consider the situation: I was a mere child who had been raised in a traditional Catholic family, my father had even studied to become a priest, yet this voice told me that the historical teachings as told by the Roman Catholic Church were false—that the religious stories I had been taught by the church, my parents, my

Catholicism classes, were not the truth. This knowledge, this entire experience, was totally foreign to my culture, to my upbringing, and to my childhood beliefs.

This voice, however, did not say that God did not exist.

But the message had an even deeper spiritual truth. I had the feeling that what this voice was really saying was that s/he did not want me to live my life in a lie, not ever. I was encouraged to question. I was never to accept anyone's belief systems without thinking for myself. I was encouraged to seek my own truth.

To question.

I have always known that I was a little different. I was an overly sensitive child at best and continue to be overly sensitive as an adult. Regardless, I was wise enough at this young age to know how my experience would likely be received; I could never prove this reality to anyone, so I remained silent. I did not utter a single word. While I never forgot the event, I simply filed it away in the far reaches of my mind, until a much later day—approximately fifty years later.

Still, on that childhood day, the presence assured me that s/he would be with me for the rest of my journey—that no matter how difficult life might appear, I could have this feeling again. Forever.

And over the years, that same essence has continued to communicate with me, periodically, playing an even larger and more prominent role in my life. Generally the communication is felt or intuited, rather than heard. Some of my experiences have been life altering and difficult to explain; others have been subtler or at least far less exceptional. Irrespective of their degree of intensity, each experience has taught me truths of how I am to live my life.

In the days that followed that initial visit with God/Spirit, I was especially drawn to wonder and questioned as much as an eight-year-old mind might, following such an intense experience: what is the meaning of life? Why are we here? How did it all start? Among my earliest recollections of this time is the memory of walking with my dog and cat down the neighbouring tractor lane to the fields behind the house and lying with both of them in the long grass, watching the clouds, and asking myself these very same questions.

It was the beginning of a very special relationship with God/ Spirit.

That childhood day in Oyster Bed Bridge became a day of firsts: the first time God spoke to me, and the first day I questioned my own mental health. And I could not separate the two.

At the time, I totally accepted the message as being real, as being natural, believing that perhaps every child received similar communications. But on another level, I must have truly questioned the ordinariness of the event, for I never spoke of this experience to anyone, ever—not even my father, with whom I shared many philosophical talks; or my mother, whom I trusted with my life; or my brother; or my childhood friends. Never before had I experienced anything remotely similar to this unusual energy or awareness, and yet I spoke not a word. Emotionally, I was ill prepared to tell anyone what had happened.

The truth was that I didn't want anyone to think that I was crazy. I knew in my heart that the experience was special, but *special* also implied being different. I felt different, I knew I looked at some ordinary things differently than my peers, but I definitely didn't want anyone else to know this. By that age, I had already seen how being different had isolated my father, who seemed not to belong to anyone. The craving to be considered normal was so powerful.

I made a conscious effort to make my difference disappear. To a certain degree, I decided to numb myself to my own experiences. So I said nothing.

It may be helpful to note that my father was different than the other men in the community, more private, more meek and mild. Initially, I thought this was how all fathers lived. He didn't attend sporting events or drink or socialize with those who did. He was a family man to a certain degree, but fiercely devoted to his work, his privacy, and his religion. He loved to read, watch old movies and the evening news, and walk… every day my father went walking, in an era when no one walked for the sake of walking. Father had a small office in our house where he found solace from the pressures of his day, and he would retreat to it incessantly whenever he was home—not to a garage or a workshop or a barn or a tavern. And he had few friends. He lived his life in a quest for silence and peace. In many aspects, my father was different.

Unfortunately, as I aged and listened to more opinions and beliefs of adults, as I looked at the world through their eyes, rather than being enthralled by my own experience, I actually became quite sceptical about the authenticity of that spring morning event. I began to question my own sanity more and more, for I was told by the conventional world of adults that normal people do not hear voices, except for psychotics, and that there was no such thing as spiritual communication with humans, to the exclusion of saints and the occasional exceptional holy person, and I didn't fit into either category. Believing and trusting in anything intangible became very difficult—such thinking went against the grain. I was totally under their influence. I was learning how to live as a sensitive person in a world that often felt insensitive.

However, there was another significant and relevant factor presiding in my life—a history of mental illness and alcoholism abided in both sides of my family tree, and I had grown up quite conscious of this. My paternal grandmother suffered from depression, and Father himself told me that he had been diagnosed with severe depression during his graduate studies. Depression also flourished in my mother's family. My maternal grandfather was hospitalized for a brief time in Riverside, the Island's only mental hospital in the 1970s. I recall only visiting him a few times, but the memories remained etched in my mind, for I can remember how absolutely terrified I was of the old grey building and the presence of the other patients. No one ever talked openly to me about Grandfather Gallant's condition. I could only reason that depression was a bad thing—something meant to remain hidden.

Alcohol abuse was a way of life for most of my uncles. I knew all too well the dangers of self-medicating for one's own issues. One uncle ended up doing serious jail time for an alcohol-related accident. He later attempted suicide. Again, few people, with perhaps the exception of my father, talked openly about these matters to a child; in the midst of such emotional turmoil and dysfunction, I was not about to verbalize that I had heard a voice that I believed came from God/Spirit and that s/he encouraged me to question. My fear of being perceived in some light of insanity was far too great.

Not all supernatural and unexplainable experiences deserved to be reviewed under the inquiry of mental illness, but, in my world, they did.

Until my childhood conversation with God, I had lived a seemingly ordinary Island life. As far as my own childhood spiritual evolvement, I was raised in an atmosphere and culture devoted to the teachings of the Roman Catholic Church. Religious observation was a way of life within my childhood home. As a child, I went to church each Sunday; later on, Saturday evening replaced many a Sunday morning. I was indoctrinated into baptism, first communion, and confirmation. My brother spent his pre-teen years serving as an altar boy.

Perhaps the greatest impact regarding my parents' religious influence on me was the fact that my father, at the age of eighteen, left Prince Edward Island for Amprior, Ontario, to study in the seminary and was six months short of being ordained as a Catholic priest when he left the obligates. Religion continued to play a significant role in Father's life. While both parents did a great deal of volunteering for their community church and parish, Father's religious influences primarily came through in the form of his intellectual interests, his love of reasoning, and his desire for meaningful and insightful conversation.

My mother's religion was simple and unquestioned. She was raised in an equally traditional French Acadian Catholic upbringing. She was mad for religion: the icons, the symbols, the mysteries, and the hope. A wooden crucifix was placed above the doorway to our living room—the figure of Christ pierced in his side, the blood hardened, and a wreath of thorns wrenched upon his head. It was one of many effigies.

Less notable than my father's stint in the seminary, but of equal importance and influence to my sense of religious development, was the charitable essence of both of my parents, who gave much of themselves back to their community. In addition to his work-related volunteerism, Father gave a lot of his free time to the church, and Mother was forever a model of Christianity. As devoted as she was to prayer and mass attendance, my mother taught me by her manners that it was all for naught if the spoken words were not put into action. Her insistence on helping others—her neighbours, her extended family, or members of her church—proved to me that at her deepest level, Mother could see beyond the symbols, statues, doctrines, and ceremonies and that she truly revered the essence of the original revelations that the Church was founded upon.

It was the genuine practice of spirituality that she was drawn to, her sincere concern for the welfare of others. Faith without good deeds was meaningless. Hers was a life of meaningful service to others. And, above all that, she truly loved everyone in her path.

My childhood religious indoctrination was comparable to my classmates' and neighbours'. In my community, like many Island communities of that time, church and school were completely intertwined. Much of the elementary education I received was at the hands of the Sisters of Notre Dame. All but two of my home-room teachers from grades one through eight were ordained nuns. The majority of religious people I encountered as a child were, to the best of my knowledge, good people. I loved the Sisters of Notre Dame who taught in our elementary school; my grade one and grade eight teachers remain particularly dear to me. The nuns were living proof that God creates all kinds of creatures, for some of these women were among the most loving, caring adults and have left blessed memories, while others were among the most bitter, cantankerous souls I have ever known.

It was within these surroundings that I first began to question religion.

After receiving my childhood message, I rebelled as much as any good child from a loving, conventional home could within reason. To begin, I refused to become an altar boy, though my brother, all of my neighbours, and most of my male classmates were. There were two or three other Catholic boys in my class who did not join, but they all had family or personal reasons that were more apparent. I would go as far as to speculate that I was the only Catholic altar boy holdout in eastern Canada who had a father who had studied in the oblates. By the end of our provincial schooling, I would be the only non–altar boy among the Catholics in my parish who graduated from high school.

Why I, as a mere child, was allowed to abstain, I have absolutely no idea. I cannot deduce why my father and mother didn't force me to conform. My mother must have been mortified. I was a shy, sensitive child, so I can only imagine that my father remained mindful and respectful of my gentle nature and convinced my mother not to force me into the public light. As for my own budding personality, I was also very set in my ways.

The greatest religious challenge of my schooling materialized in grade seven, when the government of the day decided that our smaller Island schools, regardless of religious influence, should officially desegregate.

Prior to this announcement, each morning, the Catholic kids from the area bussed to South Rustico, while Protestant children attended a one-room school in Wheatley River. That was just the way things were across the Island. I never heard any adults or children question the segregation.

When Protestant students began attending the Catholic school, the handful of Protestants in each classroom would be asked to leave during our religious studies period. What a secluded and segregated practice held within the confines of an educational institution! You invite someone to join your school community and then make sure they feel really welcome by pointing out their differences and physically separating them for periods of time.

This practice took place in the same classrooms that taught us that racism was wrong and shared stories of the Civil Rights Movement in the United States. I told myself that if even one child—and I am sure there were many—felt degraded, then our religion classes were completely hypocritical.

This integration of neighbouring Protestant students must sound desperately trivial to younger, more accepting generations, but it certainly was an issue in my day. That amalgamation served as one of the more liberating events of my youth. Abolishing segregated schooling on the Island was a truly Christian act, and it forced me to consider that all religions could be deemed equal to mine. Some of my closest friendships arose out of that blending of students. Why would I believe that my religion alone was right by the sheer accident of the family and culture I was born into and brought up by? These were normal, likeable children, and our similarities were far greater than our differences.

There was a significant degree of hidden dysfunction in our home, which I never understood until my early adult years, and not fully until after my father died. As a teenager, I didn't even know what I was rebelling against. I thought I was acting out against the conventional and conservative image my home represented. I was introduced to alcohol in junior high school, at the age of thirteen, and began drinking regularly by the age of fourteen. My behaviour was fairly reckless by choice, but I was not alone.

I was using alcohol to reach an altered state, where I could rise above my fears of conformity, believe that I was filled with love and happiness—for as fleeting as the pleasure was—and go out to meet the world. I wanted love to be my natural state but could not sustain it in the real world. I wasn't ready or mature enough to become fully aware and accept what was troubling me.

And throughout all this time, I continued to sit in church among the adults, convinced that God/Spirit had spoken to me, and that s/he had informed me that the historical teachings told by the Roman Catholic Church were false, that the religious stories were not the truth. This was the very Being that everyone around me was schooling me to believe in; however, my God/Spirit felt different. For starters, s/he was telling me to open my eyes… to question… to learn my own way to know him/her… to never, ever live my life in a lie.

Eventually, church attendance became a family struggle. I was bored and uninterested, and besides, it was an area of rebellion in which I was assured of getting a reaction from my parents. Though I never stopped believing in God/Spirit, I was, however, beginning to look at spirituality removed from the concept of organized religion.

As I trace my loss of religious faith, another event that had an immediate impact on my view of organized religion took place one Friday night during my rebellious adolescent years. As a teenager in high school, I frequently attended dances held in the upstairs of the historical Farmers' Bank back when it served as a community hall. To the right of the bank was the home of the parish priest, and then to its immediate right, St. Augustine's Church. Directly across the parking lot of the bank was the elementary school we all attended. These dances, typical of most small community adolescent dances of the times, were a source of great merriment and entertainment. We kids had a lot of fun, drank way too much, tried to hook up, and there was more than the occasional fight. In retrospect, the entire scene was quite a circus.

On one particular Friday night, a fight started between a local boy and another colourful character from the neighbouring community of North Rustico. Naturally, a crowd gathered, and just as the boys were about to square off in front of the parish house, the parish priest suddenly appeared. With his protesting arms fluttering in the air, he drew a halt to the fight before it could begin in earnest. He was a warm, good-natured, well-liked man of Acadian roots. And his protective behaviour was what I would have expected from any priest. The man proceeded to give a brief lecture on the lack of respect we were all displaying by encouraging a fight in the nearness of our historical and sacred church. No one among us would have dared to argue with this man or his reasoning. Then the proverbial arse fell out of the kettle. It soon became obvious that our parish priest was quite drunk. As we blindly followed, this man led the crowd of teenagers away from the proximity of the church to the parking lot closer to the adjacent school, and then he proceeded to encourage the same two boys to fight.

Standing directly beside me, the parish priest confessed, "I love a good fight," and he literally began to shadowbox the air.

I was speechless.

"I used to box in my day," he proudly told me.

Now, this behaviour was so far removed from what I would have typically ascribed to a life devoted to Jesus Christ. I was actually quite comfortable with the earlier lecture about the lack of respect and the order to move off—I had in fact welcomed his reprimand. However, his subsequent behaviour was the first incident in my life where I truly saw the humanity of a priest. I did not judge him, I mean that, but I began to see him as just another human being, with strengths and weaknesses, human desires and human faults. He was a normal person. He was entitled to a few drinks if he should so desire; however, I never saw him in the same light again. This experience solidified my childhood belief that I didn't need anyone, no intercessor, to facilitate my relationship with God/Spirit. That was my own responsibility.

God may very well be found in any church, mosque, or temple, but my God/Spirit was readily available everywhere, especially in people and nature. Or as Marianne Williamson so eloquently puts it in her book *Tears to Triumph*, "The only church, the only temple, the only shrine that ultimately matters is the ground on which you stand right now." A true spiritual quest is a personal, individual journey.

So for the rest of my childhood and teenage years, the only other occasions where religion felt different were the beach walks with my father. Though the subject matter was not restricted by any means to religion, it remained a special time put aside for our private conversation, and it was these talks with my father that stayed with me most. Along the north shore of Prince Edward Island, the beaches of Brackley, Stanhope, and Dalvay, I was introduced to the basic teachings of religion, philosophy, and psychology. Father's views were never forced upon me as gospel, and like my childhood spiritual message, I was encouraged to question, question, and question. No one was giving sermons from a pulpit; I was not expected to read my answers from a scribed scripture; it was as far removed from unquestioning obedience as any child could experience in a learning situation. These oceanside talks became the foundation for many of my own interests and learning that I would later develop.

And though I may have displayed an open resistance to organized religion, these talks helped me maintain a strong sense of spirituality. I always felt God/Spirit's presence around us. S/he was always there.

My involvement with the church began to erode. I accepted that I didn't believe in religion anymore, at least not in the same old way. I began to question the very rocks that my childhood religious beliefs had been built upon. Soon church attendance was limited to Midnight Mass, Good Friday, Easter Sunday, and the occasional drop-in. Eventually, I walked away from it all. It became my fundamental belief that civilization will only thrive not directly because of God's compassion but rather from women and men leading other women and men in compassionate action.

My father's people immigrated from County Caven and County Monaghan in Ireland. Though it was generations ago, his ancestry remained special to him, and he wove his forefathers' stories into his very being. The realm of mysticism and the supernatural manifested a slightly different perspective in Father's Roman Catholic Irish heritage than the more traditional Acadian religion of my mother. The Smith side of my family was definitely more open to this world, and I, too, was drawn to the curiosity for the mystical. One might think that I might have been caught between these two very different perspectives, but I wasn't. To my young ears, my father's family provided a degree of validation for my spiritual experiences. So while other children may have been entertained by ghost stories as they sat around summer campfires, the legends I was being told involved real people, anecdotes detailing Irish entities who were "gifted," visionaries, characters with local colour who could sense the unforeseen or read and interpret signs from the natural world, as in seers who could predict who in the community might be next to take their last breath. And these stories took place in the familiar surroundings of our family living room or in the kitchens of my Irish relatives.

"We were on the road heading home in horse and sled. It was cold out, snowing heavily. We had heavy blankets wrapped about us. And as we passed St. Patrick's Church in Fort Augustus, it spontaneously was shrouded in light. It was as if the interior was suddenly illuminated by hundreds of candles. And then just as quickly it returned to darkness. We all saw it. Your grandfather held the reins and turned to me and said, 'That means a certain parish member has passed away.'"

"Did you believe him?" I asked my father, who had been sharing his story.

"Of course. And it was true. We were later to learn that someone from the parish had in fact died that very evening."

"Did my grandfather believe in the supernatural?"

"More than any of us."

Father stopped to drink from his cup of tea before he proceeded to explain.

"For a while your grandfather built wooden coffins for the community, and this alone provided a wealthy source of tales and folklore. There was one time when a twin had died." Father paused to laugh. "Sorry, I'm not laughing at her death but rather at the story that followed. Your grandfather was delivering the coffin he had made to the undertaker. The man asked if Father was busy. Father replied, 'Not overly,' and inquired why. The undertaker said, 'The sister, meaning the twin, will be dead before you get home, and I tell ya I'll be looking for another coffin.' Sure enough, an order for a second coffin was waiting when Father got home."

Father, lost in memory, continued his chuckle.

"What about you?" I asked. "Do you have any superstitions or beliefs about the dead?"

"Well, I'd never enter an unlit church upon nightfall."

"Why not?"

"For fear of bumping into the caskets of those dearly departed."

Father had answered my question as if his response was common sense. I, on the other hand, found it remarkable that a man who had spent two-and-a-half years in the seminary studying to prepare for priesthood was still scared to enter an unlit church.

Who was I to argue?

My father's openness to the world of mysticism and the supernatural helped ingrain in me a sense of respect for the spiritual world. The spiritual world as it was bestowed to me was a world to be revered and not to be taken lightly any more than a seaman would ever disregard the power of the sea; however, it was not a world to be feared but to be embraced. I believe it was this acceptance and openness that gave me permission to explore this domain of the unknown and to trust my instincts and the knowledge that I might obtain from these experiences rather than to rely solely on rational thinking. His openness was my initial bridge to both worlds.

Like the world of the supernatural, intuition was an area that Mother was not comfortable with. Unlike my father, she could not be drawn into conversations of spirits or souls, clairvoyance or intuition. And there is one specific incident that stands out in my mind.

I came home one day from nowhere in particular to find my mother in an agitated state.

"Have you heard?"

"Heard what?" I asked.

"Jason and Marie's home in South Rustico had its basement badly vandalized." Mother was beside herself. "This sort of thing never happens around here. Fortunately, no one was home at the time, so no one was hurt."

"How did they find out?"

"Marie came home, witnessed the damage, and called the RCMP. The rumour is that several thousands of dollars' worth of damage has been done."

Mother was visibly shaken by this news for she knew the family and the husband's extended family quite well.

I looked Mother in the eyes and said, "The wife did it." I wasn't being smart; I just knew.

Mother was furious with me. I had never witnessed her like this. She began to shout at me. "How dare you talk of those people like that? They are good people. That's how rumours start."

"Hold your horses," I replied. "I'm not judging anyone. I know they're good people. I'm simply telling you what I believe happened."

Mother looked at me as if to say, "You have some nerve," but instead she said nothing and walked away in complete disgust, leaving me to stand alone in our kitchen, as if I had done something immoral. Her silence spoke volumes. She was furious over my behaviour.

A day or two later, the wife eventually confessed to the RCMP.

I never said, "I told you so," and Mother never acknowledged the accuracy of my insight. Instead, she acted as our previous exchange had never happened. Mother merely passed on the updated information to me, and nothing was ever spoken again regarding the matter. It was a defining moment as to the nature of Mother's and my relationship in regard to the unknown.

While university fostered both learning and understanding, it wasn't an overly spiritually defining time for me. It was not a spiritual void, but rather that I was developing more physically, emotionally, socially, and intellectually—which was all good. Outside of my beach walks with my father, university was the one domain that encouraged me to ask meaningful questions. It was the period in my life where I began to truly wrestle with the meaning of life and the role of religion, but in an intellectual as opposed to solely an emotional way. And my faith began to change as I was exposed to the teachings and beliefs of other religions outside of Christianity.

Strangely enough, it was literature like Leon Uris's classic novel of Ireland's struggles, *Trinity*, where I found a lot of early meaning. I could relate better to these fictional characters—like Thomas Larkin declaring, "We have submitted as a people to a Christ fantasy that has dulled our minds to think for ourselves and kept us on our knees pleading guilty to a terrifying God whom we are not permitted to know as intimate." Many great philosophers had said so much but not in such poetic rawness.

I had never been introduced or exposed to such controversial comments and opinions in my home or from the raised pulpits of my church. Slavery had been abolished, women had won the right to vote, and children were finally being encouraged to have a voice against abuse, but where was the voice of reasoned discourse in religion in my country? What I was searching for in religion was the right to question and to believe simultaneously. But that was never encouraged. Instead, it was literature that introduced me to this deeper analytical study, providing new lenses of the world.

All these years later, I can still recall the sense of solace and contentment I experienced when walking along the tree-lined campus, especially in a late autumn evening, amid the warm surroundings of the historical red-brick buildings, or upon entering small intimate classes on cold winter days. It was the hardwood trees reaching to the sky that brought forth the most spiritual comfort. And I found a state of awe upon reading the mystical words of William Blake—*To see a World in a Grain of Sand / And Heaven in a Wild Flower / Hold Infinity in the palm of your hand / And Eternity in an hour*—and know his feelings on some level.

If adolescence was my family rebellion, then university was my period of ethical rebellion: my true time to examine, question, and verify. But I still wanted to find my God/Spirit, so I left.

In between degrees, for four-and-a-half months, I travelled to Britain, Ireland, and fourteen European countries. For three of these months, I moved around with my backpack, travelling mainly by train, occasionally hitchhiking. I visited a church almost every day and a pub almost every night. While visiting various religious sites throughout parts of Europe and Great Britain, I came to fully accept that all of the great religions of the world were equal and worthy. I saw no reason to put my childhood religion above any other. It was the first time I had walked among so many different faiths. This was 1984. Europe was far more religiously diverse than Canada. British Columbia, on the West Coast, was far more diverse than Prince Edward Island; Charlottetown, the capital of PEI, was more diverse than the rural community of Oyster Bed Bridge. In many aspects, I was a long, long way from home. However, if I could take the time to understand and be open to my parents' perspectives, I could do the same for other people and their religious beliefs. We are one human race.

Regardless of what humans have made of religions, it was clear that all the great religions wanted the same good to come to their followers. They all wanted their people to come to know their version of God. I came to believe that no religion deserved a monopoly on this. Each individual religion was a means to know God. The issue was not whether you believed in any particular religion; the more important matter was whether a person tried to force their religious beliefs on other people.

In this relatively short span of half a year in my life, I would devote much time to challenging my thinking on religion. In the end, I came away from my travels with some very different and distinct religious experiences.

The first incident occurred early in my travels in the remote, rugged, beautiful landscape of Ireland, in the province of Connacht, County Galway. In the village of Inverin, Irish was still the language of the home. It was Saturday, September 23, 1984. I was staying at a local B&B. The proprietor spoke excellent English, and he encouraged me to drop by the local pub, assuring me that my lack of the Irish language would present no barrier. I took his advice and travelled not far down the road. It was warm and friendly, a quaint little spot that grew more crowded as the night progressed. Behind the bar, a picture of a local man who boxed in America graced the wall. I met a lad who was home visiting for the weekend. A bit of a local hero, he was an enormous man who played semi-professional rugby in England, and one of the few in attendance who spoke fluent English.

"Are you around tomorrow?" he asked.

"I am. I leave Monday for Galway."

"Drop by here tomorrow after church, for the High Mass. There will be a great session on for sure."

"That sounds great. Will you be here?"

"Definitely. Most everyone in the village drops in."

"I'm not so sure about Mass. I wouldn't understand a word the priest was saying."

Just then the governor of the village happened to be walking by; he had overheard our conversation and felt comfortable enough to interject.

"Excuse me, young man. You can pray in any language," the governor offered. "I think God will understand."

"Never thought of it like that," I replied, which I hadn't until that time.

"You go to church to talk with God. He'll listen."

The more I thought of our conversation, the more it clarified my own beliefs—though maybe not in the way the governor had insinuated. Language definitely wasn't an issue, but, for me, the reasoning was entirely different. God may very well have been there to listen to people; however, I was always more interested in trying to listen to him/her.

In the sixteenth century, Catholic nun and mystic Saint Teresa of Ávila suggested that people create a place of quiet and invite God to visit and bestow his wisdom rather than actively seeking him out; that place could be deemed prayer or meditation. On that Sunday morning in rural Ireland, as I sat quietly while about me others prayed and sang in words that I couldn't understand, I felt I could hear God/Spirit just as easily as in any church back home. The stillness I sought was more like meditation than prayer... where I left myself open to hear his/her voice. Prayer, I thought, was talking to God/Spirit; meditation was listening. God/Spirit, I deemed, had her/his own language.

On a rather cool, fall day for Tuesday, October 30, while backpacking through the country of Germany, I visited the medieval town of Dachau, and I still consider this day to be one of the most powerful experiences in my life thus far. Dachau is about ten miles northwest of the city of Munich in the state of Bavaria. My experiences in these two cities could not have been more different. Just over fifty years earlier in March of 1933, the Nazi party, which was primarily concentrated in Munich, opened the Dachau Concentration Camp in which tens of thousands of predominately Jewish German prisoners would be murdered. Dachau was the first such Nazi camp and would serve as a model for others that followed. These concentration camps would soon become known as extermination camps.

At present-day Dachau, the concentration camp is now a memorial site, and, being a visitor, I got to tour the "shower" (or gas chamber), the crematorium, the desolate bunkhouses, and a heartrending photo exhibit. I believe the stench of death and the emotional suffering of such inexcusable pain still abides there, hanging in the air. Nothing in my past could have mentally prepared me for this visit. No history lesson could ever have done it justice. I came away from Dachau and had to ask myself, *How could an all-powerful and almighty God allow such human suffering?* I knew of no religion that could explain this. My beliefs were truly being challenged. These evil men had killed a multitude of innocent people for no other reason than because they were Jewish, and because a crazed ruler had told them to do so. Surely these men, these killers, could not have been made in God's image as my church had taught. It was not on this day that I began to question the validity and sincerity of organized religion; rather, on this day, I had to question God/Spirit's existence. Our relationship was being tested.

Munich, on the other hand, was determined to move along.

Europe was a constant stream of stimulation—seeing new places and doing different things. My intuition was strong. Strange coincidences continued to happen.

Less than a month later, on November 14, 1984, after travelling through parts of southern Germany, Austria, and Switzerland, I arrived on an early-morning train in the historical city of Rome, Italy. Another traveller and I had arrived at the Rome Termini, the main railway station. We got off the train and immediately set off to find accommodations. We were approaching the nearby traffic circle, Piazza della Repubblica, when I noticed three backpackers heading towards the train station. One person had a Canadian flag on her backpack. I had reasoned that they had just vacated a room, so I approached them regarding possible accommodations. This was about to be one of the biggest synchronicity experiences of my trip.

Two of the backpackers were a couple, and as I spoke to them, the third person, a girl about my age, was looking at me intently. After I had gotten directions from her companions, the young lady approached me.

"Are you from Prince Edward Island, out around Cavendish?"

"Yes, I am. Are you from PEI?" I asked excitedly.

"No, I am from BC."

Now I was really confused.

"So how do you know where I am from?"

"I celebrated my eighteenth birthday with you, your friend Marcel, and a group of my girlfriends at the pub in Cavendish."

"Wow."

"I can prove it."

The girl anxiously proceeded to open her backpack and took out a small purse-size photo album.

"I have been showing these pictures to people I've met for the past three months. I've been seeing your face." She turned towards the back of the album. "See. There you are with your friend, and that's me."

Sure enough, there was my best friend, Marcel, and myself surrounded by a group of girls in the Cavendish pub. It was a source of much amusement among the group of us as we gathered on this foreign street corner. The world seemed so small and intimate.

As they prepared to leave us, my new friends informed me that Pope John Paul II was giving an audience that very morning. "You should check it out," one of them said as they waved goodbye.

As I had hoped, we were able to secure their newly vacant room. My travelling partner wasn't interested in seeing the Pope, so I threw my belongings in a corner of the room and ventured out alone, figured out the bus system, and arrived at the Vatican with little time to spare… only to be stopped by security at the entrance gate and asked for my pass. *What pass?*

This was also the point in my life when coincidences began to take on a richer meaning.

The young man doing security was dressed in traditional Roman garb, and he spoke quite good English. I explained my situation. Discreetly, the guard handed me a pass and whispered to me that while he searched my daypack, I was to present the pass back to him as if I had just located it in a pocket. Of all the security guards at the Vatican, I was fortunate enough to get this understanding young man.

Within minutes, dressed in the cleanest of my dirty laundry, I was seated among the well-dressed audience who had been waiting anxiously for the Pope. But there was more. As fate would have it, on this very morning, among his various blessings, Pope John Paul II was giving a special blessing to Canadian visitors. In fact a large portion of the audience was made up of Canadian tourists (who had arranged many, many months beforehand for their seating).

As the Pope left the stage and walked down the aisle, I was no more than twenty feet from him. I still have the photo to prove it. I had never been in such close proximity to anyone who commanded such reverence and admiration. The energy in the room was both addictive and electrifying, and it was clearly an atmosphere of love. It was obvious that the audience was deeply moved by the presence of this holy man.

This was a world so far removed from the greyness and misery of Dachau.

Those two distinct experiences, my visit to Dachau and to the Vatican, could not have been more different.

I knew I was meant to be in that audience. I was questioning my religion and yet against great odds, I got to be in the presence of the most valued person of my childhood religion. I found peace here for a reason. It would take years before the teaching was revealed.

Part II

We can't have full knowledge all at once.
We must start by believing; then afterwards we may be
led on to master the evidence for ourselves.

Thomas Aquinas

The only real valuable thing is intuition.

Albert Einstein

IN THE SPRING OF 1988, at the age of fifty-eight, Father decided to retire. He was tired. He felt it was time to go. Then the faintest, most subtle signs—brief lapses in memory, a lingering headache, and changes in his mood—began to appear. Initially, I was convinced that it was a case of severe depression. Father went to see several doctors, and they, too, thought it was depression. Then, his physical balance began to leave him, and there were intense moments when he had trouble verbalizing his thoughts.

Then the greatest of coincidences happened.

Doctor Gill, a well-respected Island doctor, who had had cancer himself, heard about my father's condition. The story that has been passed down to me is that someone had approached Dr. Gill and spoken to him about my father. While travelling through the countryside one day, the doctor followed his own intuition and stopped by the family home. He literally just came to our door, introduced himself, stood in our kitchen, took one look at my father's eyes, and diagnosed him. He knew it was a brain tumour.

Within days my father was transferred across the Northumberland Strait to Moncton Hospital in the neighbouring province of New Brunswick. Father was diagnosed with a malignant brain tumour, and the tumour was embedded. Within days, he was transferred again—this time to Saint John, New Brunswick. Time was of the essence; Father could not afford to wait.

I am not sure what would have happened had Dr. Gill not stopped at our family home; I am sure that his visit did result in the extension of father's life and that he was meant to call in to our house. I do know that some of my most powerful experiences and memories occurred in the coming months.

"Was it worth it?" my father asked me, as he lay in his hospital bed.

It was the night prior to his operation. I had no idea what he meant. I was completely caught off-guard and confused by the perceived boldness of the question. "Yes. Yes, Father, it was worth it," I managed to answer.

I was twenty-six at the time, and this event marked the end of much of what I had believed about my childhood. It would also serve to become the event that marked how my relationship with my father would drastically change.

Father's four words—*Was it worth it?*—challenged my entire belief system.

The truth is I had hoped that the answer was yes, and that at least part of the answer was standing at the foot of his bed.

My father had survived the operation, but it was not successful. One morning, against my mother's wishes, I took Father for what would be our final walk together along that distant shore. I thought it would be healthy to give Father an opportunity to verbalize any thoughts and fears regarding his pending death or to voice any concerns he may have been harbouring. I gently approached the subject. "Dad, what do you think happens when we die?"

As I describe in *Finding Forgiveness*, he began to speak to me of love:

> *"The purpose of this world, this life, is love. And there are different degrees of love."*
>
> *Speaking was difficult and proved to be too frustrating. Spying a piece of driftwood, he picked it up and used it as a means to overcome his verbal obstacle. Being physical helped Father organize his drifting thoughts. He drew three individual circles in the sand; though detached, the circles were arranged above each other: Father's conception of the stages of love. The first circle, on the bottom of the arrangement, represented the love of friends, our social interests, and communities. A higher love, the middle circle, was the type of love he attributed to his wife—and I feel secure enough to suggest his immediate family. The final circle was reserved for the greatest love he deemed available to humanity. Beside this circle, he traced the word "God" in the soft, moistened sand.*

I share these two conflicting images from my father's last days on this world, his dark night of despair before his operation and the obvious love he held for his God as depicted in his circles in the sand, for both events have impacted my own belief systems with as much rigorous affect as any of my early childhood teachings. These contrasting events occurred within the span of four months, the last four of his life. Those four words—*Was it worth it?*—continued to play out repeatedly in my life, often taking on new meaning and significance at various stages; however, the image of those three circles has had an equally significant impact on my overall growth and spiritual development.

In early October, after a short stint in the local hospital, Father was transferred to the Eric Found Centre, a hospice unit. For ten days, our family took turns keeping watch, assuring that my father's soul would not leave his body without someone being present. There was never an extended period whereby his hand was not held, or an accompanying voice was not speaking or captured in prayer.

This dark, decrepit building, so grey and gloomy, would be condemned within a few years. Yet, despite the prevailing heaviness, the hospice truly felt like a home; and it, too, was filled with a beautiful emotional and spiritual energy. More than merely cope, the staff excelled. These caring and compassionate women displayed a genuine respect for everyone who entered the premises, patients and family members alike. They instilled a model of integrity and serenity that was spiritual in nature.

October 10, 1988. A host of family members gathered about my father's bed. I observed the sacred rite: the formal act of anointing my father's body. A moment heightened with emotion as my father's ordained brother performed the ceremony, an observance in preparation for death. Prayers were read aloud above his weakening heart, for my uncle had always preached that the devil waits to take a dying soul. And in the early hours that precede dawn, I witnessed my father take his last breath.

The halls of the hospice were dimly lit. Seeking solitude, I wandered away from my father's room and found myself in small nearby family waiting room. The rising sun cast enough light that auxiliary lighting in the darkened room was not warranted. I was familiar with this modest chamber and easily made my way over to the seasoned couch that lined the wall to the left of the doorway. The only other piece of furniture, in addition to an aged standing lamp, was a leisure chair that resided in the corner to the immediate right of the entrance. The chair was partially hidden from view by my opening of the door; it only became visible as I closed the door over.

I became aware of a silent presence sitting behind the door, leaning slightly forward in the chair. And by the silence of his manner and the hour of the given day, I felt void of any need to engage in conversation or even to acknowledge this person's presence, for there was no part of me that was not consumed with loneliness. The paradox of my emotions: awaiting the reprieve from the suffering that my father endured while simultaneously bearing an unparalleled anguish of loss. I had never known such intense grief. My anguish came from deep within, and cupping my head inside the privacy of my hands, I wailed. I was, as Tennyson described, "an infant crying in the night… and no language but a cry." At death, we become as children.

Following the intensity of that brief moment, I no longer wished to be alone. My soul was craving companionship; I now welcomed the presence of my silent companion. His company had provided a sense of security and the freedom to grieve openly.

Then the door opened, and my grief was gently disturbed. I looked up to see a family friend, who upon witnessing my moment of grief, smiled, and departed as discreetly as he had intended to enter. Though fleeting was the light of the hallway that penetrated the doorway, that crept ever so briefly into the room, it shone long enough to let me see my surroundings.

The chair was empty; no one was sitting upon it.

It would be years before I would as much as speak of this incident, and then I did so only among a few strangers. It was those close to me whom I alienated. I felt no need to share this experience, for I knew all too well that my words could not be validated and the risk of how my words might be received. I admit that I equally felt no need to verify the authenticity of my experience. I was not alone.

There is simply so much more to this world than our minds can comprehend.

The Greek word for miracle is *simaios*, which means *signs*. The Oxford Dictionary defines a miracle as "a surprising and welcome event that is not explicable by natural or scientific laws and is therefore considered to be the work of a divine agency." These experiences are not only for mystics, but also for the miracle of everyday life.

I got to truly know my father only after his death.

A few days following my twenty-seventh birthday and the burial of my father, my mother called to tell me that she was ready to begin to go through my father's belongings. I had made plans with Caitlin, my girlfriend, and had decided to proceed with these plans. However, as she and I were leaving the city and I came to the "Y" intersection at the edge of town, where veering to a sharp left would take me to out to Middleton and Caitlin's family and driving straight led to Oyster Bed Bridge and Mother's, I received a message: something was wrong at home. It was a sudden, intuitive awareness.

"I have to go home," I said.

"Why?"

"I don't know. I just have to."

I could not explain it. Something beyond my understanding was at play.

This day would prove to be a defining moment in my life. On that quiet, sunny afternoon in October, I altered my plans for no concrete or rational reason, drove out to my childhood home, and walked inside from the warm autumn weather, and life as I had known it changed forever.

As I entered the family home, I witnessed my mother holding Father's briefcase in her arms. I watched her lay the briefcase on the kitchen table and set her fingers upon the metal clasps. I knew that she wasn't supposed to open the briefcase.

"Don't open that!" I blurted out.

The contents of the briefcase would prove to me that my father was homosexual. At that moment, I left my body, my knees weakened, and I broke out in a sweat. I was now outside of myself, looking down from above, looking down upon myself. I did not feel any emotion, but it was as if I saw myself feel. I was overwhelmed and anxious. What I do know is that during that time, I was no longer Adrian; I was more than just my body; I was more than my feelings and emotions; I was somehow beyond it all. Those emotions were real, but that was not who I was. I was a soul witnessing that I was anxious. For that moment, I was separate from my story. Then, as if I was guided, I entered Father's office and knew exactly where to go and what to look for.

I invaded the privacy of Father's desk drawer, where I found two large, plain brown envelopes that I had never noticed before. I held the packages, turning them in my hands. The ends were stapled shut. One package had a simple message written upon the top: *Personal Property.* I tossed it aside. The message on the second package was more articulate: *In the case of my death, please destroy without reading.* I had no intention of opening the packages; I knew that no good would come of it.

There was additional implicating proof in this desk as well as the one at his office. I told myself that I would begin by destroying the evidence. That night under a cloak of darkness I drove to the community dump, drew a wooden match across the rough surface of a rock, and lit a fire, adding each individual paper, each envelope, and each solitary magazine to the flame and watched the smoke curl and rise into the night air. I burned the privacy of his words.

From the time of receiving the message until I burnt Father's personal papers, someone, some unexplainable force, was guiding everything.

I made the decision that day to not tell a soul about my father's past while my mother was alive. I felt that I had been given that responsibility. I began to live my life as if it was my sole duty to protect her. It was both the time and the culture I was living in:

No one talked openly of homosexuality in their families.

I had no history to draw from.

No one in my circle talked about unexplained messages either.

Therefore, I kept that information inside me as well.

This entire experience would prove to be the greatest test of my spiritual awareness as, initially, I allowed the spiritual aspect of that event to simply become part of the overall secrecy—every aspect got rolled in together. As long as I continued to deny the implications and significance of this spiritual experience, the other domains in my life remained equally stagnant. On the primary or physical level, I felt betrayed. My father had lived a lie; therefore, I believed that all major aspects of my life must have been a lie as well. Then on the spiritual level, my recent experience of receiving a message simply defied reality. All of my previously held beliefs were being shaken. Everything was up for questioning.

I had experienced a moment of mystical proportions, yet my ego rejected this. Even in spite of my childhood message, the old, logical part of my mind still kicked in and lodged a complaint. I found it difficult, almost impossible, to believe what had actually happened. Even in the face of the spiritual significance of the event, I was overwhelmed and could not move beyond my personal sense of loss. I was not ready, nor was I willing, to reflect on the importance of the experience—to truly see the world through my father's eyes or even to look at the larger world picture through a more spiritual lens. I allowed myself to be consumed with mundane, everyday fears.

I had been given an opportunity to know love at a deeper, richer level, but I had not yet learned to walk in the dark. It would be many years before I could see this experience in another light. My experience of this experience would change; I could eventually use it to broaden my essence of love, find an unknown blessing.

My world could never be the same; someone, some force, some entity had literally reached down and changed the course of my life—but I could grow and evolve because of this experience. In due course, I would; however, it would be years, many years, before I could see beneath the surface of appearance to a deeper truth, to truly understand and accept this experience as a lesson in love. The world was offering me a lesson on love, but my eyes were closed. Life lessons do not always come in perfect packages.

I was well aware that accepting the enormity of what had happened, both the unexplained experience and the resulting family knowledge, not only changed my life, but could dramatically impact the lives of the people I most loved in it as well. Almost immediately, an internal debate arose and continued to surface almost every time I reflected upon this happening: *Why me?*

And then so many other questions surfaced:

- Why did I receive the message and intervene?
- Why not my brother? He was older.
- Why not my mother? She was the caring protective parent.

- What was the true reason for the intervention?
- Was the intent solely to protect my mother or was there a deeper, more meaningful purpose?
- Receiving messages from the unknown does not happen every day, at least not in my experience. I was directed to intervene. Why did I do so blindly? Why didn't I question?
- Does this type of event happen to others? No one has shared similar experiences with me that I can recall.
- Do I tell anyone?

This was the first of many examples of compelling irony: on the day, I was driving along innocently when I was directed to go home, and I did so obediently, without question. In fact, there was an overwhelming urge to obey. Yet, the first message that I ever received from this same source was to always question.

I asked myself, *Why did you comply?*

The answer: because this incident felt realer than real. I had heard what I could only describe as an undeniable inner voice. It spoke with such purpose and authority. The message was a directive, the message was explicit: I had to go home. I believed that if it wasn't a truly significant message, I wouldn't have heard it in the first place. My greatest act of faith was in trusting that message.

Still, it was hard for me to accept what had transpired. Intuition is not logical. It's an awareness that goes beyond what our minds can perceive.

And somehow, just somehow, that proof, that degree of evidence that only I am guided to find, subconsciously justifies in my mind why I tell no one; it justifies why I don't ever question my intuition afterwards.

I am a fan of Swiss psychiatrist and psychoanalyst Carl Jung, the founder of analytical psychology. I was especially fascinated to learn that Jung had always believed that spiritual experiences were essential to an individual's well-being. I was equally intrigued that Jung, however, was honest and candid enough to acknowledge the degree of stigma and ridicule that was often associated with the telling of these experiences and how carefully these secrets tended to be guarded. Jung was a highly regarded psychologist, and he presented a vicious real-life dichotomy... for through his professional work, Jung understood the prevailing attitude of ridicule that existed in regard to spiritual experiences while knowing full well how lethal keeping secrets could be for his patients.

Jung was correct.

On average, people with personal visionary accounts are generally not taken very seriously by society. I needed not to look any farther than my own past behaviour as to how I tended to respond to others' personal stories, which I confess was somewhat less than accepting and leaning much closer to judgemental. I did not want to subject myself to such ridicule, yet I could not deny that my experiences had a powerful and lasting effect. This was a path in life that I was not willing to venture into lightly. I was reluctant at best. In time, I came to believe that psychic occurrences were actually quite common and not restricted to the lives of mystics and mediums. What was rare was people's willingness to tell others.

Regardless, the dichotomy that Jung addressed still existed in my own life.

I believe it must be rare when people actually endure such unexplainable experiences and then go back to their regular lives without some major changes in perspective. Whether or not I decided to speak of the happening or not, this event was life-changing for me, and it would prove to be essential for my future well-being.

Part III

*A simple glimpse of heaven is enough to confirm
its existence even if it is never experienced again.*

Abraham H. Maslow

Intuition is Spirit knowing Itself.

Ernest Holmes

AFTER MY FATHER'S DEATH, it was only natural to question what happens when we die.

Where would his soul go?

For as religious as the man was, the subject of the afterlife was a topic that my father rarely spoke of. I do know that he did not believe in a traditional Catholic version of heaven and hell; however, he did believe that our souls carried on... that as in the Buddhist tradition of karma, people would be given other opportunities to grow and develop—though he rarely, if ever, spoke to me of reincarnation. His view of the afterlife was rather that life forms continued to exist on other levels or domains of life.

I recall one of our earlier father-son walks along the north shore, when Father avowed, "There will be no lying around in the next life. We will still be working and finding purpose and meaning in our lives wherever this may be." Then later, after Father drew those three circles in the sand, this conversation regarding the afterlife took on deeper meaning.

If we believe in Albert Einstein's brilliant work on quantum physics, then we believe that while energy actually turns into matter, essentially energy cannot be created or destroyed; it can only be changed from one form to another. So I began to ask myself: Where would my father's energy, his spirit, go? Had he completed his life lessons? Would he be reincarnated to try and try again? Or was there another domain in which he would live?

If our world could be divided in halves forever and ever, could infinity not go the other way? Could our universe, our world, expand beyond depths that I could not imagine?

I didn't have the answers, but, as usual, I had a lifetime of questions.

Life has taught me that if you bury a lie deep in your subconscious, you bury other things as well—and some of them are good. When I tried to suppress my anger and shame, my ability to feel excitement and zest for life, to be playful, to laugh, and to be creative was also diminished. Abraham Maslow has said that often when we try to protect ourselves against the hells within us, we also cut ourselves off from the heaven within. The heaven within that I was losing was my spiritual connection.

It was the first instance, and there would be others, where my intuition would suffer; I received no further direct communications for years, and my spiritual experiences were no longer heightened. To some extent, the emotional turmoil of my present life had blocked my spiritual awareness. In my anguish, I was the antithesis of being open and receptive to experience; I may have been silent, but I was no longer listening. I had to heal the splitting of myself.

These were harsh realities for me to accept, but even my secrecy back then proved to be a significant spiritual lesson to me. I had to accept that I was no more forthcoming with my unexplained spiritual experiences than Father was in revealing his homosexuality. For different reasons, both of us feared negative perception and open rejection. Yet, I criticized his silence.

How my life, much like his own, would have been different if I had been more courageous and less insecure.

Over the course of the ensuing years that followed my father's untimely death, I continued to receive many wonderful lessons. Not all of my spiritual teachings were supernatural or found within the confines of scripture or poetry. In fact, God/Spirit's presence was best found in simple, common, and ordinary ways. Some of the finest teachings were from those beautiful, enlightened people who continued to surround me—various people who would weave in and out of my daily life. Though the conveyance and context of these relationships varied greatly, the message was always the same: the meaning to life was love.

Corey was my first godchild. He and his older brother were raised in Calgary, Alberta, by my first cousin Michelle and Michelle's parents. Between the year of his birth in 1985 and Corey's initial visit to Prince Edward Island in the summer of 1991, both my father and Corey's grandfather had died, both deaths the result of cancer. I was well aware of the sense of loss that Corey was experiencing, for his grandfather had been by far the strongest father figure in Corey's young life.

By family standards, the summer of 1991 was magical: it served as a family reunion of my mother and her three sisters. With two of the four being recently widowed, the emotional support the sisters were able to provide for one another was enormous. Their energy was heartwarming and intoxicating. Lazy summer days were spent idly at the beach or in laughter at family gatherings; evenings were a continual source of entertainment as we shared many meals and had drinks together while telling stories and playfully tormenting one another. The days seemed to flow into one another.

On the second-to-last day of Corey's visit, a large group of us had spent the afternoon together at the beach. It had been especially warm that day. Drained by the combination of heat and high energy, I had gone back to my mother's house to cool down and have a nap before supper. Mother, who had elected to avoid the summer heat, was home when I arrived.

"How was the beach?"

"Excellent."

"Will you be joining us for supper?"

"Yes, but I'm wiped. I have to go lie down for a bit beforehand."

I excused myself and ventured upstairs to my old bedroom.

Mother sensed that something more was wrong. No sooner had I lay down than she was knocking on the bedroom door.

"Is everything all right?" she inquired.

Without any warning, I began to cry uncontrollably. Nothing of that sort had ever happened to me before. If asked, I could not have explained my behaviour. Then I began to ramble.

"I'm so worried about Corey. He's heading home, moving so far away. I know that he has people who love and care for him... his mom, his grandmother, his Uncle Michael, my Uncle Leonard, good neighbours... but he has no father, nor grandfather."

Mother stood, leaning against the doorway, and smiled—a behaviour, I remember thinking at the time, that seemed liked a very peculiar reaction to my obvious discomfort. She pushed away from the doorframe and began to come closer.

"Do you know what is happening?" Mother asked.

I shook my head no. I had no idea.

Mother drew near my bed.

"It's the first time in your life that you have truly fallen in love with a child."

Still I said nothing.

Then she sat down beside me and took my hand in hers. "Isn't it the best feeling in the whole world?"

When Father left the sacred confines of seminary life, he began a career in education, teaching primarily in rural one-room schools broken by a short stint at an inner-city school. Leaving the priesthood was a monumental decision; in spite of the assurance by the Monsignor that "there are many ways to serve God," teaching was never quite enough. Father was looking for more, a link between the humanity of teaching and the spirituality of ministry. Counselling would prove to be the perfect middle ground. It was a safe bridge.

Father claimed counselling was a calling—a calling to make a difference in people's emotional and family lives. He was prepared to be a caretaker of other people's souls. He believed counselling was an admirable profession, one that was aligned with his moral teachings. His new vocation would be spent in passionate service to helping solve others' problems.

I, too, had always known that I wanted to be a counsellor. Some might say it was in my blood—on my father's side, I came from a long line of "wounded healers." I can honestly say that I had always been drawn to the idea of understanding human nature and more specifically the meaning behind human behaviour—two prominent conversation themes of my childhood beach walks with my father. But far greater than that, my inner voice always believed that counselling was also my own spiritual calling. I only had to listen to what the author Marianne Williamson calls our "divinely inspired guidance system," and I knew that I would not go wrong.

After five years of teaching, I made the transition to fulfil my calling and moved to Fredericton to study at the University of New Brunswick's Master of Education program to specialize in counselling. Going back to school at thirty was a big move for me. It was a big move financially, and I was also mentally struggling with the idea of being a "mature student": how was I going to fit in?

Returning to university proved to be a marvellous experience. The more I settled in, the more I loved being back in a university setting and the more independent study approach of the Master's level deeply appealed to me. I was confident that I had made the right choice, that I was on the correct path, and I enjoyed the friends I was making.

One of the highlights of my year involved a chance meeting with one of my professors. The weather was particularly nasty this early winter day, and, as I had walked to school, I had elected to stay inside our main building and kill some time between classes. Noticing me lingering, this professor invited me to join him in his office. He immediately went over to his bookshelf and took down a relatively small, thin book.

"Have you ever read *Man's Search for Meaning* by Viktor E. Frankl?" my professor asked as he passed me the book.

"No, I haven't."

"You should. I think that you'll get a lot out of it."

I was already overwhelmed with the degree of suggested and required readings associated with a full university course load, and my expression likely said as much. In addition, I was beginning the research component for my thesis. It seemed like I was forever reading counselling based material.

The professor noticed my hesitation.

"I realize that there is a lot of reading in this program. I'm as guilty as the next professor. But, Adrian, you already instinctively know a lot about counselling. It's obvious. This book will do more for you than any textbook reading you are going to encounter, even anything I will ever assign you. I suggest that you pick up your own copy because you will be referring back to it forever."

After class that same afternoon, on my walk back to my basement apartment, I stopped at the campus bookstore and purchased a copy of the book he had so passionately recommended. The book sat on my desk for a few days, until the weekend when I was able to set aside some unobstructed time to begin reading it. From the very beginning, I couldn't put it down. I read the book in a few sittings. No book had ever had that much impact on me. Furthermore, my professor saw something in me, and he took the time out of his day to chat… to be open. That chance encounter had by far the greatest impact on my academic year. It was one of the finest examples of pure education. This reading had absolutely nothing to do with an assignment or some future exam question. Rather, it was the mere sharing of knowledge for the pure sake of knowledge. This professor trusted that I would be learning at another more meaningful level. I am forever grateful for his interest in me.

The term *wellness* was relatively new in the early 1990s. Back then, the general public was still inclined to think of health in terms of physical health. My thesis was entitled, "The Relationship Between Wellness and Self-esteem Among Adolescents." I wanted educators to think of health as the result of all the biological, psychological, and social factors in a person's life—the integration of body, mind, and spirit. I wanted to incorporate spirituality and Maslow's self-actualization as much as I could into my literature review; I longed to take as true of a holistic approach as possible. I wanted to include spirituality in my actual study. I believed that spirituality was the core—the creative force of the human system, and that for complete harmony, balance, and wholeness, a person needed to be aware of his or her concept of spirituality.

Most of the studies in my research pertaining to adolescents were willing to include the concepts of self-actualization and stress management, along with the basics of exercise, nutrition, interpersonal relationships, and health responsibility, but back then few studies recognized the importance of spirituality, especially with this age group. Neither did my university program. I was forced to limit my scope, to conform. Spirituality was not included in my study.

In the summer of 1992, I returned to the Island, having already accepted employment as a school counsellor with the former Unit Four School Board. The following school year, I would be based out of Morell Consolidated School and would travel to three additional small neighbouring schools. Such assignments were affectionately known as "the milk route." For the time being, the emphasis was on completing my thesis. It was my intent to complete as many chapters as possible before the new school year and my new career began.

The rustic little one-bedroom cottage was situated in Rusticoville along the bank of the New Glasgow River. The cottage was hidden from the main highway at the end of a dirt lane that gently sloped down to the edge of the water. I was renting the place from an aunt of one of my closest friends, and it soon became a haven of sorts. The pace had been quite hectic in Fredericton as I was anxiously finishing up my studies. Here I was surrounded with only peace and tranquillity, the lull of the water sweeping in towards the house.

No cable or satellite television, not even a phone on site. I had to ask the landlord who lived in the neighbouring cottage to use her phone. It was definitely the solitude that I had been seeking.

The next spiritual highlight and teaching of my life transpired with the birth of my second godchild, Chantle, who was born in August 1992. Chantle is a sibling to my first godchild, Corey. This time, my mother and I were asked to be godparents. We were honoured. That winter we flew to Calgary, Alberta, for the baptism. My brother was also living there at the time, so it was an added pleasure to spent time with him.

In the days preceding the baptism, I spent hours with this beautiful child. One of my favourite photographs ever is of me resting in a recliner while Chantle sleeps peacefully upon my chest. That baptism, where I held that innocent child in my arms while water was poured over her head, assured me that there was an interconnectedness to this world. For I knew that day that she was part of me.

Many of the spiritual truths I learned, I learned from watching others.

While I was struggling to come to terms with my father's past and my damaged relationship with the church, Mother made a change. She woke one morning knowing something was different. She was different. The truth was that she had been changing all along; I just didn't see it coming. I'm not sure that she did either.

Widowed with an empty nest, Mother found herself overly settled and conventionally bored. I'm not sure many people antici-pated this change, as Mother always favoured her routines; however, now she wanted more, a life further outside of herself. Somehow, she found the courage to take the risk and began volunteering at the hospital. In the present day, with so many successful women in politics and the work force, volunteering must sound pale in comparison, but for Mother, volunteering was her middle ground, providing a renewed sense of purpose that had been absent in her recent life. For one day a week, there was an extra special reason to get up and get going. And of all places to volunteer, she selected the section of the hospital where they examine for breast cancer, and there had been so much cancer in her family.

"Wouldn't your mother want to distance herself from the cancer ward?" her friends would ask me in private. Others would declare, "I don't know if I would want to be reminded of all the cancer."

Some would question her directly, and Mother liked to inform these people that the examinations are preventive. Preventive became a key word for her. She likely heard the term during her training, liked the sound of it, and held on to it. She knew that she was making a contribution through her kindness.

The people she greeted at the QEH, for the most part, were new to her. Mother was widening her circle of compassion, extending her kindness to the well-being of strangers. In her eyes, she had been denying herself her wholeness by not giving to others outside of her extended family and immediate community. It took effort on her part. She was lonely and lost and could have elected to stay home, to while away her hours feeling sorry for herself. Instead, she transcended these negative thoughts and behaviours and sought out purpose and meaning. I believed in my heart that the work was therapeutic, that it was helping to heal her soul.

One night we were speaking on the phone, and I was just about to say goodnight when Mother started up the conversation again.

"You know, love, volunteering is my private means of saying thank you. It is how I can show the gratitude I feel towards the nursing staff for the compassion they showed our family when your father was ill."

I knew all too well of the power of gratitude. Her words were like music to my ears.

"I'm glad you find it so rewarding."

"If I can give the nurses a bit of a break by doing the small stuff, I figure they'll benefit more than having another picture on the wall."

At the age of thirty, prior to our meeting, Cheryl had had breast cancer. Being a single parent and having had to face the fragility of life at a relatively young age had renewed her appreciation for living each day to the fullest. I believed that she had taken a good, long, and hard look at her life and had made some concrete decisions as to how she wanted to spend her remaining days regardless of how many there might be. There were more important things in life than a tidy house. Her concept of what was important in life had changed. Her vitality was infectious, irresistible to me.

Cheryl also saw potential in me that others couldn't see or that I had successfully hidden. We had a turbulent journey at the beginning, but where I had provided others the right to doubt me and they had willingly accepted this challenge, Cheryl never wavered. She saw me for what I could be. She believed in me. Unbeknownst to me at the time, Cheryl was offering a foundation, the safety to be my own true self.

I had my only experiences of healing energy with Cheryl.

Her family had a history of back issues, primarily herniated discs. One evening early into our friendship, I was visiting with Cheryl and her young family out in their home in Warren Grove. Cheryl was complaining of having a sore back.

"I can't afford to be off work," Cheryl said, and, by the intensity of her voice, I knew she meant it.

"Prepare yourself for bed," I asked her. I had no idea where my thoughts were coming from, but I knew that I could help her. "I'm going to help with your back. I just need you to relax and go to sleep."

After the children were in bed and Cheryl had settled, I asked her to turn towards the window and I climbed in next to her with my clothed body pressed against her back. I wrapped my arms around her and simply held her. I remember looking at the moon through her bedroom window and saying absolutely nothing. It was a feeling that I cannot put into words; it could only be felt.

The next morning, Cheryl woke and her back felt great, and though I had hardly slept, I felt totally refreshed. It was all energy, but it was an energy that I couldn't explain. But later, back at my apartment, I was absolutely drained, and I slept for most of the day.

For anyone who has ever had cancer or loved ones with cancer, you know the importance the medical profession puts on the first five years. During that time, it is a common tendency to view every new symptom in light of *has the cancer returned?* We were no exception.

Cheryl had been scheduled for a biopsy in the coming days. During her last examination, her doctor had found "irregular patterns" in her breast tissue. She was concerned, and her face couldn't hide it.

At the time, I was renting an apartment in a beautiful part of town off of Victoria Park. It was a lovely place for Cheryl to retreat to when she had a free evening. She would come visit, I would buy wine, and she would cook us supper. Sometimes she would play the guitar and sing while I did some writing. We were comfortable in each other's company. This night we were sitting in bed, our pillows stacked against the wall, and I put my hand above her breast. The energy was intense. We sat there for ages without saying a word—neither one of us wanting to question anything.

We couldn't tell if anything was happening. It just felt different. There was a strong energy between us.

The following week she went in for further tests. When the results came back, the doctors couldn't explain it. There were now no traces of the irregular patterns.

"Sometimes these things just happen," Cheryl was told.

Sometimes things do just happen.

Cheryl and I never really spoke of either incident afterwards.

What would we say? That our energy healed her?

I definitely never considered sharing this experience with anyone. I knew only that our energy was different on those nights. You could not convince me otherwise. It was yet another example of the unexplained energy connections that this world has to discover.

I believe that some places are more spiritual than others. For me, I need to be surrounded by water. I need only to go inland to feel disconnected. Outside of Prince Edward Island, I had never felt more at home than along the rugged coast of Ireland. It has been a spiritual haven for me. I feel so connected there.

Cheryl and I travelled there in the summer of '94. It was Cheryl's first real holiday without the children. The opportunity to be together alone was enough in itself. I had also accepted a new job, which would be starting in September, so we were both in an exceptionally good place. I had visited Ireland on my own ten years earlier and had always desired to return.

But this was all new for Cheryl. She brought such a full and exciting energy to such experiences that many others, I'm afraid, might take for granted. She savoured every moment we travelled together.

We had landed in Dublin. The B&B was nothing special, other than it apparently was referred to in James Joyce's *Dubliners,* so once we got settled and showered, we went for a grand walk about the city, visiting St. Patrick's Cathedral, Christ Church Cathedral, Trinity College, and Grafton Street. The young girl at the tourist office actually knew where PEI was located because of *Anne of Green Gables.* I gave the young lady my version of Anne to which she readily compared an Irish leprechaun.

There were street musicians everywhere.

As we rounded a corner, I heard the most beautiful music ever. It stopped me in my tracks. A young lad was playing the uilleann pipes, which I had never seen or heard before. The musician was shy and made no eye contact with the crowd, only modestly thanking someone who dropped a coin. The sound was ever so haunting and spoke to my soul. Never had music touched me in such a powerful and moving way.

"Welcome back to Ireland," my spirit seemed to say.

Slea Head is the westernmost point of Ireland; nothing stands between it and home. We drove by bus from Dingle, passing the "Sleeping Giant" along the way. There was a point in the road where a stream ran right across the road; crossing it divides you from the veil of the ordinary to the spiritual. A stone crucifixion statue marks the entrance to Slea Head, followed by the encompassing view of the Blasket Islands—nothing short of mystical. Wildflowers grow alongside the stonewall fences, cobbled lanes, and cliffs. The bus driver actually dropped us off at the BB's door.

I spent the early hours of the evening simply watching the weather change as various layers came in across the horizon. That night I could not sleep. There was something about the energy of the place that was both overpowering and unexplainable. I did not want to go to sleep in fear that this feeling might escape. Still, I woke the following morning feeling fresh. The only other time I had experienced anything remotely similar was back on the Island, in Warren Grove, when I had wrapped myself around Cheryl in an attempt to ease her back pain. Once again, it was a feeling that I could not put into words; it was an energy that I couldn't explain; it was a force that could only be felt.

The Aran Islands, off the west coast of Ireland, are a quilted patch of stone-fenced fields, squares of manual labour, with land rich from hand-drawn seaweed. The pastures spread outwards to the summit of a vertical cliff face. From the musical haven of Doolin, if the day is clear, you can actually see the islands off in the distance. Cheryl and I eventually landed on Inishmaan, the largest of the islands. Nary a word of English was heard as Irish was still spoken among its people. We walked the ground covered with early Christian sites, a hallowed land rumoured to be littered with the graves of saints. The remoteness and beauty of the land alone lends itself to prayer.

The weekend we arrived was one of festivity, a homecoming of sorts, as a young bride had returned to the comfort of her village home for her wedding day. Several of the villagers stopped us as we walked about, inviting us to the *craic* that was as certain as nightfall. The lady at the bed and breakfast recommended what she deemed was the better of the two pubs and suggested that we might eat a little later the following morning as she and her husband would be out rather late, likely into the wee hours of the morning. She was talking my language, so I was more than willing to oblige.

The pub we entered, typical of many in the midst of Irish celebration, was saturated in traditional music, rounds of laughter and drinks, and much local character. Many of the villagers, who now lived off of the island, had returned for the weekend wedding, bringing the English language with them, and within the presence of their voices, our sense of ease and familiarity grew. We were welcomed into the fold.

A group of musicians had gathered in a corner of the pub; the sounds of several fiddles, guitars, a bodhran, tin whistles, and the rhythmic stepping of shoes rolled through the wooden building. Occasionally a voice would accompany the wind and strings. Cheryl nestled in among the musical gathering while I wandered about, a Guinness in hand, snooping like a lost dog for sounds of spoken English. Having made my rounds, I eventually returned to find Cheryl, guitar resting upon her lap, singing a ballad with the locals, and the mere sight warmed me.

Her main accompanist was a schoolmaster from a small village outside of Galway who, like many, returned home to Inishmaan each summer for vacation. During a pause for refreshment, he and Cheryl sat to one side, and he asked all about her: her family, her occupation, and her likes. Amidst their friendly banter, sharing impressions of each other's countries, the schoolmaster asked, "So what religion be you?"

Cheryl, who was just raised her glass to her lips, paused her drink to answer. "Oh, Adrian is Catholic, and I was raised Protestant."

"Protestant!" As if stricken of the very air he needed to breathe, he gasped, "I can't believe it."

Being too flustered to retain his composure, the schoolmaster excused himself. Cheryl remained seated, isolated, looking somewhat bewildered, feeling completely lost. The man whom she had befriended eventually returned and took his seat alongside her. He looked her directly in the eyes. Rather than apologize for his behaviour, the schoolmaster said, "I can't believe it. You're such a lovely girl. I have a daughter who is not far from your age."

Cheryl got up and left immediately. She caught my attention and drew me aside. She was shocked—no, rather, disillusioned. In broken speech, she shared what had just transpired, and tears eventually came to her eyes.

"He rejected me because I'm Protestant?"

Instinctively fearing that I would be torn away from both the music and the Guinness, I immaturely asked, "Why in the name of God did you tell him your religion?" I had been coaching Cheryl on the very subject, preaching never to speak of religion.

"What was I to say? He caught me off guard."

"Lie! You're in southern Ireland, you're Catholic. What difference does it make to you? You don't even go to church."

"He was so nice. What difference could my religion make?"

It was an honest and fair question. What possible difference could her religion make? How could Cheryl possibly be more appealing had she been born into a Catholic family? She was warm and friendly, beautiful, musical, a caring single mother; how could any humane person base her worth solely on the religion of her ancestors?

Because of his ingrained belief system, this stranger felt justified to judge Cheryl based solely on religion.

We finished our drinks and retraced our steps to the B&B. The good of the evening had been taken from us. The ruins of a church were barely visible in the dim light of the moon. Much of what remained of the ancient Catholic Church lay below the earth's surface. I paused and looked down from the rim of a sunken wall. The liquor had loosened my tongue and caused my mind to wander. I looked at the ruins, then at Cheryl, then to the pub off in the distance from which we had travelled.

"You know, Cheryl, my father was months away from his ordination, and I can proudly say, the man never saw a difference. The religion you were raised in, the colour of your skin, your nationality, your gender, or your sexuality never made a difference. He accepted everyone."

I wanted so much to tell her all that night and to share the beauty of my father. Unfortunately, the power of the lie was still too great. I could not share about his homosexuality.

Cheryl and I were determined to see Northern Ireland as well and not be dissuaded by the history of the Troubles. The local papers were full of coverage of the previous day's meeting in Letterkenny regarding the IRA and Sinn Féin. The general consensus in the articles was the inability for the IRA to be reasonable. We didn't know what to expect from our travels north.

What we found were a people and landscape every bit as beautiful but with far more trees and a pace of life even more to our liking, a part of Ireland much removed from the tourism of the south. Derry was the first city we visited and by far the friendliest, most helpful town we had visited thus far in Ireland. There was a pub in Derry called Bound for Boston; this intrigued me, as this was the route for many of my ancestors as well. The last night in the city, we landed in O'Donnell's for a grand traditional session. My fears of travelling north had proven to be a waste of energy.

The next day, we were a little worn out when we landed in Malin Head, another remote beauty, and stayed at the Crossman's Inn. We walked around the head of the peninsula, the landscape changing every so often. It was amazing. That evening after supper, though it was July, the proprietor of the inn made a coal fire in the sitting room. After a bit of reading, I slept in a big armchair for over two hours. The comfortable chair, the heat of the woodstove, the deep sleep, it all reminded me of being in my Aunt Cis's country kitchen. Then we even had biscuits with our tea before the fire.

That night I wrote in my journal:

Tuesday, July 26, 1994
Malin Head

It is simply amazing how things can come together. When
we are in the mood for something, it just occurs. We wanted
music and came upon a great session. Today I needed rest
before our last few days, and the Inn was ideal. I just have
to let it happen, let life unfold, rather than always be in
search of something.

Back on Prince Edward Island, I had one of the strangest sensations
that I have ever experienced.

It was mid-August now, and Cheryl and I had been back from
Ireland for just over two weeks. In preparation for the coming
September when I was starting a new job and knew that I would
be exposed to a vast range of counselling-related issues, I decided
to stop by a local bookstore and seek out some relevant reading
material. I did not have anything specific in mind; I just wanted
something handy in case the mood to study came upon me—something to break up the end-of-summer beach reading.

I took my time, browsing through the psychology section, reading
the various titles, but nothing was jumping out at me. Then, without
any warning and for no tangible reason that I can explain, I suddenly
felt an intense sensation. My head became light, and I thought that
I might faint. The only time I had felt anything remotely similar was
when I left my body while being guided to find Father's personal
writings in the sanctuary of his office. This time the exceptional
number of pertinent titles—incest, suicide, bereavement, addictions, sexual abuse, and dysfunctional sexual relationships—had

seemingly overwhelmed my brain; the list seemed to go on and on and on. The complexity and the abundance of the available literature greatly disturbed me, and my mind began to race. Then just as suddenly, in the midst of all that confusion, I experienced an entirely new sensation. For a brief moment, as if time stood still, it looked as if all the books before me had meshed together, as if all those themes—addictions, abuse, and dysfunctional relationships—had the same derivation, which was an unknown to me.

Then my attention was instantaneously drawn to the bordering section—that of spirituality and religion. It felt as if my eyes had been suddenly forced open, and yet, simultaneously, it felt as if I had known this teaching all along; I just hadn't been listening.

It is difficult to give physical descriptions to non-physical events, to put the experience into words. But once again, it was a moment of awareness, of personal insight—the message being that the true nature or purpose of counselling was to be viewed from this deeper, spiritual perspective and awareness.

Without purchasing any book, psychology, spirituality, or otherwise, I immediately left the bookstore, feeling somewhat shaken. I was simply too startled. In my heart and mind, I believed the message. It felt like I was being called to an awakening, but I was refusing the call. The depth of my insecurity and need for conformity were still far too great.

Our brains are also wired for conformity.

From an evolutionary or Darwinian perspective, it's really not survival of the fittest individual; it's the most cooperative community of species that endures. In essence, common beliefs help take care of our genes. Like most people, I elected to take the road most taken.

Like my other spiritual encounters, the bookstore experience never left me, and, from time to time, I would reflect upon the incident. One of the primary related struggles I was enduring was that I still equated spirituality firmly within the well-defined confines of organized religion. Even the book section was entitled "Spirituality and Religion."

Though I never made any drastic changes in my outward life, these experiences had a tremendous impact on me; their memories were never far below the surface. I would allow myself to be amazed by these experiences, but then my ego would click in, and I would try to explain them away. I knew that I was different because of these experiences and a different person than who I would have been had I never had such experiences, but I made no immediate or external effort to change my behaviours or practices; I spoke to no one of my experiences; I did not begin to attend any religious or spiritual classes, groups, or lectures; I didn't even change my reading preferences. I simply continued on my personal journey and tried to remain open to future teachings.

What a walking dichotomy I was.

The third time God/Spirit spoke to me was in the summer of 1996.

I was working in the remoteness of Guyana, in South America, having volunteered in a program of international development to work with the relatively untrained teachers within this isolated region of the world. As part of my training, I met my team in Ottawa where we were introduced to each other and participated in sessions that dealt with cultural awareness and sensitivity. Then we travelled as a group, arriving first in Trinidad, the Caribbean island off the coast of Venezuela. When half a day had passed, my team boarded yet another plane and flew farther south into Georgetown, the capital of Guyana. The locals call it "Garbagetown" and with good reason. There was garbage, everywhere.

We were given two weeks to settle, to acclimatize, before an open boat carried us across the vast water of the Pomeroon River Region. An awaiting Land Rover drove us even deeper into the hinterlands, to the foothills of an amazing rainforest. The secluded village of Charity is literally the end of civilization. Only the wilds of the river and forest lie beyond the sanctuary of its modest harbour.

There were six of us in all, Canadian teachers, all strangers to their ways. It was my first real taste of being a minority. We had all volunteered to share our teaching skills. My role here was that of a counsellor, a keeper of secrets.

The school more closely resembled a barn than any institutional building I had ever known. The lights dangled aimlessly, taped along the exposed wooden structural beams that tied the ends of the building together. The outside shone through the worn openings in the boards that formed the bases of the walls. The rainy season had just arrived and already the warm rains poured out of the skies, tapping then drumming upon the tin roof, drowning our foreign voices that hung in the open-aired classrooms totally void of sound insulation.

This structure was a home to six hundred students on any given school day. The building was justifiably condemned. Portable blackboards, faded and worn, were shared among classes and barely readable. Textbooks, when they did exist, were outdated or laid about in wretched states, having been passed down from hand to smaller hand well beyond their time. Void of telephones and televisions, it was a learning institution in want of computers, in need of overhead projectors and photocopy machines. It was a world denied of the technology that we, North Americans, took for granted. Despite all its deprivations, it was proof that teaching can occur in the direst of surroundings whenever there is a willingness to learn.

My father had a saying, "Do not devote a life to knowing others until you come to know yourself," and as I walked those clay-packed roads of Charity, I would often wonder what he would have thought of his son deep in this remoteness, driven so far inland, so far from his home, preaching self-respect and spiritual harmony to audiences who struggled to decipher my darling Island accent when there was so much of myself I still had to know.

Charity was a climate of acute poverty and despair that conflicted with the overwhelming beauty and benevolence that prevailed. The animals were thin and roamed freely or lay idly along the unpaved highway. Living conditions for many were destitute. The people had little money, and there was even less for them to buy. It was a country in immediate need of sanitation and health care. Bottled water was a way of life for us, and the mosquito netting that lined my single bed was a constant reminder of malaria. The villagers shared their food, their smiles, and their music—their community. Deprived of common domesticated conveniences and comforts, these spirited people drew from within and from each other, creating their own instinctive forms of merriment and entertainment. Song and dance, storytelling, and plays were natural means of expression and communication.

It was their love of the water where I could best relate.

I have always lived within an arm's reach of water and have always associated this feeling with home. I need only to move inland to feel the pangs of separation and divorce. To these native people, the sea was their arteries of life. They took of their food from within its depth, drew meaning and essence from its being, purpose upon its waves, spirit in its wake. I remember watching as a young child, as young as nine, with a bare back, no life jacket, and knowing no fear, paddled an open canoe over waters of the depth that allow the passage of large sea vessels. I came to learn that his father's hands had carved that canoe from the body of a single hardwood tree. The people bathed openly along the river's edge, and, in the evenings, the women would cluster to gossip and tease while they washed their family's clothes by hand.

One morning a man slightly older than me stopped me while I was walking. He proceeded to question me as to how my home country of Canada could threaten to separate over a mere two languages. He invited me to look around, assuring me that I would see diverse races, languages, and religions working in harmony and sharing their space. While this observation was especially evident in the community market, where it had held even more significance was at the local church.

Not far from the school stood the one church in the village, and it was Roman Catholic. The local people explained that the other religious denominations around Charity were too small and poor to afford a church, so the Catholic Church allowed other religions to use their church. That alone was so beautiful. However, an even greater surprise awaited me when I decided to attend church on Sunday morning, and, to my amazement, a woman was saying Mass. There were not enough male priests in rural Guyana to get out to the remote parishes, so the congregation had decided to ask this nun to say Mass. I had the pleasure of speaking with her afterwards, and she was indeed a special person, as holy and spiritual a person as I had ever met. It was an honour to talk with her, to be in her presence.

This experience was an extension of my childhood acceptance of Protestant students being integrated into our Catholic schools— again, how could I possibly believe that one religion, one sex, one race, or even one country could have more access to God than another?

This was a good period in my life. I was thirty-four years of age and was thriving on this sense of adventure, full of purpose and meaning.

I had been in Charity seven days. When that second Sunday arrived, as faithfully as dawn, the village radiated, captured in brilliant fabrics of vibrant colours, stone jewelry, hand-carved crafts, and woven goods, and the visuals and smells of tropical fruit, foods I had never known to taste. It was their cultural version of the farmers' market. I wandered through the morning hours, through the throngs of people. Streets were impassable as locals journeyed inward from the neighbouring countryside to barter or exchange their wares. I watched a stream of people arrive by foot, mule-drawn carts, or different fashions of boat. By mid-afternoon, the spoils of exposed meats and fish heightened with the lack of refrigeration. By evening a sense of restlessness gradually began to surface with the coming of dusk. The night air would soon fill with the excitement and vices of a carnival as music and laughter and drink flowed out from the tavern windows and poured onto the streets.

It was late when I removed myself from the excitement with the knowledge that I had to teach the next morning. My room was small and by relative standards the window even smaller. I lay in bed and listened to the life of the village as it flowed in from the street. I was in awe of these ingenuous people. Above my bed, a fan clicked in symmetrical fashion. I was much too awake to sleep, so I grabbed my journal and reread the notes I had been scribbling along the way. The random passages that I had written down back in July, back within the concrete and structure of Ottawa, now took on greater relevance. So much had transpired in so little time.

"Cultural awareness—being human, it is likely that we may be well advanced in our thinking in one situation yet be considered naive in another aspect of the world or environment."

Already, in the short time span of four weeks, we teachers had proven to be no exception to this governing rule. Foreigners to this enchanting land, we were well educated within our own standards, but we could not deny how much more at ease and attuned these native people were with the life that had been given to them.

In this land, removed from television and other gadgets, the onslaught of electrical stimulation, our senses had already evolved. Our senses of smell, taste, hearing, touch, and sight were heightened. Everything was so new. Though none of us had confessed this reality, the truth was spoken in the comments and observations we shared among ourselves. As our physical senses intensified, I believe so did our minds. Removed from the layers of distractions, our thinking and our reasoning became clearer and less muddled. For the first time since my father's death, I felt truly in touch with myself.

Eventually, I put my journal away and fell into a deep sleep.

"Jesus," I cried aloud to no one.

I was sitting upright in bed, my body drenched in a heavy sweat, as if a wave of fear had washed over me. I was instantly alert. Something happened that I could not bring to consciousness. I reflected for a minute, for I was unsure of my whereabouts; confused until the mosquito netting that draped loosely about my bed grounded my senses. I was alone and aware, knowing that three thousand miles away on Prince Edward Island, my mother was ill. Only moments before, distance might have appeared as a mere illusion. Now it took on a physical dimension, an unbearable reality. It dawned upon me that I had no immediate means of contacting home. The romantic remoteness of this stilled village suddenly was unnerving.

"Don't lose it," I heard the sound of my voice speaking aloud.

The clock on my headboard read 4:10 a.m. Guyana time. My

experience felt so real, so significant, that I felt compelled to write it down. I instinctively knew that my mother was trying to contact me. My journal was lying open to the left of my bed, resting on the wooden floor beyond the boundary of the meshing. Recording my experience served another purpose, for even within the immediateness of Guyana, I was aware of how my story may be perceived back at home. The fears of rejection and judgement run deep, and the need of acceptance had followed me into the sanctuary of Charity. I recorded the date, the time, and the event:

> "It is Sunday, July 21, exactly one week into my stay at Charity. I have had the most powerful experience of my life to date. It transpired in the form of a dream, but no, it was not a dream, for there were neither visions nor images. Rather it was an acute awareness, a message. I awoke at 4:10 'dreaming' (for a lack of a better word) that my mom was trying to contact me. I had a vivid sensation that she was ill."

The following morning I had a cold shower, then dressed and walked out to the common room and my waiting colleagues. I was visibly shaken. One of them asked, "My God, Adrian, you look awful. Were you out late?"

"No, it's my mother. She's ill."

"Your mother?" someone asked.

Then without listening to my story, another of the group spoke up. "Adrian, you must have been dreaming. You likely got too much sun yesterday, out on the water."

"No, my mother is sick. I can feel it."

I just knew it. Despite how strange my behaviour may have appeared, I knew this was not in my head. No matter how physically far apart we were, I knew it. There was no question. God or some intelligent source had told me that my mother was ill. No one had to convince me that what I had intuitively known was true.

My intuition had not been as strong in recent years, but the magnitude and intensity of this situation, my mother's health, had broken through. I still had two full weeks in South America, plus the journey home. I decided that I could not ruminate on the message regarding my mother's health; it was all out of my control. I couldn't explain what had happened any more than I could explain the other mysteries of my life. I didn't worry about explaining the experience to anyone, who because of their belief systems, simply would not believe this could be possible. I just trusted it was true and let it be. So instead of worrying, I turned my focus to the matter at hand, my work mission in South America.

Returning to life on Prince Edward Island was not easy. Removed from the recent diversions—the repudiate feelings and emotions of poverty, abuse, and despair—a prevailing sense of hopelessness continued to wash over me. If asked, I could not place a finger on one sole incident though the assimilation and accumulation of everything was overwhelming. Back at home, I felt aimlessly adrift. The simplest of events could trigger an emotional reaction. The size of the home I was renting would easily house five Charity families. Then there was the expense of my new Toyota truck parked in the driveway. It was all guilt. The waste of our North American lifestyle got to me. There was such an overriding sense of happiness among the people of Charity. Still, the injustice on so many levels weighed on my consciousness. The thoughts and memories just kept coming.

When we had flown into Georgetown, from the plane I could see a series of horse shelters clumped together in the distance just outside of the city limits. When we were leaving Guyana, we drove through this very same area. There were people living in these dishevelled shelters. They were not stables. They were people's homes. The heavy rains would run human waste into the streets; it literally ran down the front of these homes. Children would walk within these streams of waste. Disease and despair were everywhere, and AIDS was spreading like wildfire among the people.

One of the students in my class was a kind and troubled woman. One morning she arrived early. Her face was badly beaten by her own husband's hands. She shared her story, and though I had heard similar accounts before on our own streets, it was the look of loss in her eyes that moved me. Here I was giving a talk on respect and for days those battered eyes never left me. I'm talking of respect, and this lady had absolutely no one to turn to, no health services, no police supervision. She went to a retired priest, she told me, and told him of her situation. The fool told her to go home to her husband, telling her that if she was a better wife, her husband would not have beaten her. I called him a bastard. She left her husband by the end of our first week. I don't know for how long. The local program supervisor got wind of this. He told me another week like this and I'd either be mayor of Charity or they'd hang me in the streets.

Another young girl, no more than seventeen or eighteen, already teaching, educated by their standards, stayed after class to show me her fresh flesh wounds, raw welts where her mother had whipped her because she was seeing a young boy, poor and of the wrong religion. Apparently, I had not fully escaped the faults of organized religion.

The second week, during one of my sessions, another lady interrupted my lecture. "Sir Adrian," she called out, "you are trying to teach us to love and respect ourselves." It was like it was a totally new concept for many of the women. Initially, it was hard for so many of these women to think of trusting me, a male. There was no greater honour that could have been bestowed upon me than knowing that one of my students, who was expecting at the time, named her child Adrian after me.

The locals did not openly complain, yet there was no financial future for these people. Those who were educated left. You couldn't blame them. They learned then yearned for a life that they hoped was removed from poverty and abuse. They continually longed for something better.

The day I was leaving Georgetown, a local teenage girl had a baby. The child died, and the young mother threw the baby into a pile of garbage. Other children were watching and laughing as if it was a game. One of the little boys got scared and ran to tell a young American street worker who later came to speak to me. The young lad was a complete emotional wreck. At that moment, I truly knew what it meant to speak of taking on the suffering of others. There was just too much cursed suffering and pain. I left myself open to this stranger.

Within days of returning home, experiencing that difficult reentry, I went into a mild state of situational depression.

It was during this time of depression that my mother came to visit. There had been something she had been meaning to share, but she hadn't wanted to bother me when I was so far away from home, and then with me not feeling well upon my return, she had decided it could wait. My mother had developed a bit of an infection in her stomach while I was gone. She had been on medication since July 24, three days after my premonition, when she first went to see her family doctor.

That morning, I was lying on a couch in the kitchen, and Mother was sitting nearby in a chair.

"When did you first become aware of the pain?" I asked her.

Mother did not hesitate. "The Sunday morning previous, I awoke to an unbearable pain in my stomach." Her left hand, which was free of her cup of tea, instinctively cupped her stomach, and then circled slowly, her fingers slightly pressing against her body. "It occurred coming on morning, just after 5:00. I'll never forget it for as long as I live."

Nor will I ever forget her words.

My dream had been lost in the midst of my depression, and now the memory of that night in Guyana came back to me. I excused myself, ran up the stairs, and within the mess of a partially unpacked knapsack, a string of clothes, and travel keepsakes, I located my journal and searched the pages for a heading of July 21. There it was in print. I was amazed. I returned to the kitchen and read the passage aloud to Mother.

Then I said, "Guyana is in another time zone, one hour behind Prince Edward Island. That would have made it 4:10 in Guyana; 5:10 on the Island."

It was as if we had experienced synchronized pain.

It was a brief moment of confirmation.

Mother's reaction was immediate. My mother was sick. That much she already knew; however, for various reasons, what she did not like was my knowing. She lowered her cup abruptly and tea spilled from the rim, flowing over onto the kitchen table. Troubled by my reading, she sprang from her chair.

"You know I don't like things like that." Her voice spoke of fright and disgust; she reacted as if God had played some trick.

I wanted to inquire what "things like that" she was referring to, but I held my tongue. Instead, I watched as she headed off into the pantry, listening as she rinsed the stains from her teacup without a spoken word, the water running longer than need be. She returned with a dishcloth in hand.

"Sorry for scaring you, Mom. That wasn't my intent."

The dishcloth circled in a fury of motion on the wooden surface, soaking up the miscellaneous spots of displaced tea. She straightened her back, exaggerating the arch, and spoke to me without turning.

"I know, love. I know. I overreacted." She had embarrassed herself. "I guess I'd better be on my way," she said as she smiled while tossing the damp cloth at me and walked out the door.

This experience was evidence, once again, that the voice instructing me was truthful and trustworthy. In reality, the communication, the instinctive knowing, that I had to drive to Oyster Bed Bridge to intercede on my dead father's behalf was far more mystical, but I had allowed my feelings of shame and fear to interfere and to block this acceptance. While both events were personally validating, this recent event was different. My ego was not going to fool me this time. I had documented proof and another person's confirmation.

The other message being reinforced, once again, was that in my mother's eyes, my gifts were wrong. This was the person I loved most in life, and she held such a strong opposing belief.

In the months that followed, I spent a significant amount of time with my mother; we were always close and likely would have spent time together regardless, but everything had changed. The entire Guyana experience encouraged me to make every waking hour with Mother as meaningful as possible.

"Telesomatic: the prefix, tele, means 'distance'; somatic means 'of or relating to the body.' Together, they mean something that influences the body or the surface of a body from a distance," writes

Dr. Larry Dossey in *Healing Words: The Power of Prayer and the Practice of Medicine*. He highlights the following conditions in telesomatic experiences:

- People are not trying to use their connectedness;
- They cannot control these experiences; and
- They are not even aware that these experiences are going to happen.

According to his research, a number of premonitions target people or events, which demonstrate a high degree of entropy—meaning that a significant degree of energetic change is taking place. Dossey expands on this theory, saying that premonitions are more likely if the target "embodies some emotional significance and personal importance." Premonitions, Dossey states, "are overwhelmingly related to survival—of ourselves and of those we love." Evolution.

All of these factors were relevant to my experience.

I never felt comfortable calling the experience in Guyana a dream. Even when I initially documented my experience in my journal, I never described the event as a premonition. I did not predict the future; the truth is I became aware of an event simultaneously as it occurred—it was truly a telesomatic or non-local event. My initial description was that I had experienced a remote knowing, an acute awareness, or a message. I did not choose this event, nor did I choose to receive a message while driving my car. I did not will these events; they were beyond my control. I was naturally predisposed for these events. In both incidents, I was relying on wisdom far greater than my own.

It required a tremendous faith to accept these experiences as truths, as there was no practical explanation for why I suddenly knew something—something unknown, which would later prove to be extremely meaningful to me. The power of those particular experiences was so great that if they were never to happen again, my perception of life would still be permanently altered. Still, this was a reality that did not belong in my current interpretation of our world. In truth, they ran contrary to my views at that time.

One might question why this communication does not occur more often or why it only occurs in certain circumstances or why seemingly to some people and not others. The honest answer is I do not know. I can only speak to my own experiences. What I do know is the spiritual growth is not linear; it is a multilayer process that ever ends.

All I can truly say is thank you: thank you for lifting the veil, if only briefly, and changing my life forever.

After returning from Guyana, my intuition was stronger than it had ever consistently been before. I tried to understand why Charity had opened up my channels:

There was a void of electronic stimulation.

I was enclosed by water and nature.

I was surrounded by warm, compassionate people.

Newness and adventure kept me living in the here and now, fostering a sense of mindfulness.

I was living with a renewed sense of purpose and meaning.

My volunteer work had a spiritual disposition.

I was living in both extremes: connecting, meaningful relationships and solitude.

Regardless of any particular reason or a combination of these factors, the truth remained that my intuition had been heightened, and this reality would repeatedly play out throughout my days in the coming months. The coincidences and unexplainable events kept occurring.

Towards the end of that summer, I received a subpoena to appear in court. I was asked to testify in a sexual abuse case. The night before, I had a horrible sleep. I kept dreaming of students from my work whom I knew had been abused, in particular, this young girl who was heading to court the following morning.

The next day, I showered and dressed for court and headed into the city. When I arrived, the young girl's lawyer was standing outside of the courtroom waiting to meet me.

"Sorry to have troubled you. The case has just been settled. The offender pleaded guilty."

"No problem. That's great news for the family."

"For one thing, the police only recently tracked down one of the main witnesses."

"Really."

"You!"

"I was in South America for most of the summer."

As I was about to leave the courthouse, I met the young girl who had been sexually abused, the same girl who had dominated most of my dreams the night before.

The young girl rushed over to me and grabbed my arm like an old friend. "Mr. Smith, I dreamt of you last night. It was really weird. You were helping me, but everything had double meaning or something."

Or something.

It was early one Saturday evening, and I was relaxing in the hand-woven hammock the beautiful people of Charity had given me as a thank-you gift before I left. Anchored between two maple trees, I swung about and decided to create my own meditation.

Looking up at the beautiful maple tree in front of me, I visualized myself as the tree and that I was a child of God/Spirit, that his/

her power came through the earth, through me, and that through my own love I could reach outwards and touch as many people as possible, as if they were leaves on a tree; we could all do that. I began to visualize people: my mother, Cheryl, her children, Hayden, my godchildren, my friends, and everyone at work. Then I thought *all of these people could only be one leaf if I truly believed that we are all children of God.*

Afterwards, I felt totally relaxed for the first time since being home.

Eventually, I left my comfortable nest and ventured into the house, and grabbed a book I had started to read some time before but had since put down. The book was *Creative Visualization* by Shakti Gawain. I opened up to my bookmarked section: "Meditations and Affirmations." Gawain was writing about grounding yourself and imagining a cord connected to your spine and reaching down into the earth. "If you wish, you can imagine that this is like the root of a tree, growing deep into the ground." The energy of the earth flows through the cord and through all parts of your body.

The similarity in our meditations was too close to ignore. I felt that I was on the right path. My energy came from God/Spirit, and the energy flowed both ways.

Summer was ending. The last weekend before returning to work was upon me. I had stopped by my school to check in. There was a letter in my mailbox from a local government agency. Hell, I didn't want to open it yet; I was heading to Halifax for the weekend, for a last hurrah. I took the letter home unopened.

The next morning as I made my morning coffee, I noticed the letter lying on my kitchen table. I decided to open it. The letter concerned a student I had tested last spring. The parents were legitimately concerned, but they knew I was on holidays; there was no sense of urgency.

That afternoon, I jumped in my truck and headed for Halifax. I decided to take the ferry. Who did I meet on the boat but the parents of the student who was the subject of the letter. Having opened the letter and read it that morning, I was mentally prepared when I met these people. The three of us sat down, had a coffee together, and discussed their son's schooling in a very friendly, informal setting. It was perfect. It didn't feel remotely like work; it felt like talking to friends.

After a summer of unexplainable happenstances, I made the conscious decision one day that, unbeknownst to them, I would randomly test my intuition skills on a student. A new student had transferred to our school, so I knew next to nothing about her. While the female student sat across from me and spoke, I simply tried to remain open to any insights that I might receive about her. Then I got a hit.

During a lull in our conversation, I asked, "Do you look a lot like your mother?".

My grade eight student giggled and replied with a smile, "Not a bit. Wait to you see her. We don't look anything alike."

I felt like a fool. I apologized for disrupting the flow of our conversation and encouraged the student to continue where she had left off. We talked in general terms for a while: how she was adjusting, fitting in to a new school, having to make new friends.

Then she paused and said, "Why did you ask about my mom?"

Embarrassed, I shrugged my shoulders and answered, "Nothing, really. Just curious."

The young lady began to speak again, but after a few minutes she paused again. She was quiet for a moment while she looked intensely at me.

"I'm adopted. You didn't know that, did you?"

"No, I didn't," I answered.

"That's really strange."

Again, she was quiet for a moment; it was obvious she was pondering deeply on some matter, which I could not figure out.

"I look exactly like my natural mother when she was the age that I am now. And that means so much to me. I could take in a picture to show you."

"That's okay," I answered. "I believe you."

"How did you know that?" she pressed, but I continued to downplay the situation. How could I explain that the information just came to me?

After our session, I was uncomfortable with how that situation had played out, and the thoughts of what this student might share afterwards with her family or friends troubled me. I could have damaged our relationship and my reputation with my selfish entertainment.

I had to ask myself, what was my motivation in using my intuition? Was it to lead to love, understanding, and/or forgiveness? Did it have a purpose or was I merely playing games?

I truly believe that psychic energy or gifts are part of evolution and growth. Without any connotation of religion, I believe intuition is connected to individual and species survival and the enhancement of our essence of spirituality. It is an advanced part of our own consciousness, a higher way of relating and obtaining knowledge. I also believe that expanding the intuitive part of us is a spiritual law or truth—but like all means of authentic self-actualization, it is intended as a means of helping others. The most cooperative community of species endures.

Spirituality encompasses psychic energy but is a higher level yet.

Some messages were harder to receive than others.

I had been seeing a student for counselling. I was concerned about her, as she was very anxious, but I elected to follow her lead, not pushing her, allowing her to gain confidence. Initially, she came to see me because she wanted to learn independence and had been using me as a sounding board. The girl did not seem at immediate risk; it was her future that concerned me.

Monday, September 30, 1996
South Rustico

Last night, I had an unnerving dream, basically a nightmare. I was rushing out of the house, and then decided to return for a cassette tape I had misplaced. I ran upstairs to find it. Something else was on my mind, and I was agitated.

As I was about to leave my room, I noticed something or someone tucked in behind my dresser... hiding. Realizing it was a person I had happened upon, I got startled and began to defend myself. I clutched the person's hair and threw a punch before I was able to acknowledge that it was one of my former female students. She was in fact an older sister to the student I had been so concerned about earlier in the day.

I woke up from the mournful cry of my own voice.

The day following my dream, the mother of these girls dropped by the school. She was concerned about the younger daughter, my current student. A male classmate had recently harassed her. The mother was very bothered and wanted to talk about her fears of this boy becoming an abusive adult or of her daughter being a potential victim. She was not comfortable with how her daughter had reacted to the situation.

These two particular sisters closely resemble each other. The girl in my dream could easily have been my present student in later years. I could not explain the meaning for why she might be hiding in my room, or my reaction. The best I could reason was that it represented my failed attempt to protect—that by following her lead and not pressing or confronting this girl, I was not what she required; she was asking for help; she needed more than a listener.

Returning to work that fall, I spoke to the occasional school group or individual class and gave a few presentations to staff on my experiences in Guyana; however, not once did I mention my dream in Charity. Though the experience was realer than real, I still never spoke of the dream to my friends, as I continued to neglect to share any experiences regarding communications about my father.

A person would have the right, the insight, no less, to question: Why would God/Spirit talk to me? Why bother speaking to that lad when he doesn't appear to be listening?

The truth is that I was listening.

I heard God/Spirit the first time.

I was just too damned scared to tell anyone.

I was overwhelmed.

My experiences didn't make sense to my rational mind.

I lacked the confidence to share.

I felt I left home every time I ignored my inner voice or denied my spiritual experiences, which meant that I was denying who I truly was.

Part IV

And ever it has been revealed that love knows
not its own depth until the hour of separation.

Kahlil Gibran

Mankind's greatest gift, also its greatest curse,
is that we have free choice. We can make
our choices built from love or from fear.

Dr. Elisabeth Kübler-Ross

THE NEXT CHAPTER in my spiritual journey was highly influenced, in varying ways, by Mother's diagnosis of terminal cancer.

The medical tests taken in early summer of 1996 had shown no results to speak of. Then early in the new year of 1997, when my mother was fifty-eight years old, the results of another round of tests determined that Mother did, in fact, have cancer. The cancerous cells had been discovered in the fluid sample extracted from the "bubble" on her abdomen. Some initial surgery was required so the doctors could determine what exactly they were dealing with. The diagnosis was not great. Ovarian cancer. The medical team was only able to remove minuscule fragments of a tumour, but the primary source was elsewhere, likely in the lining of her body's walls. This explained why the X-rays and body scans failed to identify the source. It was now up to the oncology team to determine whether chemotherapy and/or radiation would be the treatment.

Mother was then transferred from the surgical unit for patients' recovery to the unit across the hall that housed the gynecology section of the hospital. At the time of my mother's stay, this maternity unit had fortunately been spared the states of grief and depression that were more common on many other units. Feelings of pride and joy and excitement carried from the adjoining rooms into the hallways and radiated from the faces of the new parents, family members, and friends who pressed against the glass partitions looking at the babies. Older siblings ran excitedly through the corridors. Even the nursing staff was not immune, and their warmth and sense of hope were gratifying. I would linger in these hallways coming from and going to Mother's room, watching the expressions and feeling the joys associated with the power and beauty of a newborn life—there is no greater energy in this world.

I would stand there knowing that an open hallway separated the cries of new life from the suppressed fear of death. It was the first time in my life where the idea of reincarnation held any meaning for me. What if my mother was to die, be reborn, and eventually come back to earth as a child; to leave one hospital room only to return to another, a room full of love and joy welcoming her back?

I would just stand in the corridor, think, and absorb the energy.

In the months that followed, I ignored the power of my spiritual experiences. My mother was ill; my work was demanding; I fell into the ruts and routines of everyday life—existing mode. If my mind was left to itself, it would retreat to old and familiar patterns of beliefs, and doubts would surface. As I allowed myself to slip, my intuition diminished.

Intuition is something we all possess to varying degrees, but you have to pay attention to it, honour it, or it, too, wavers.

It was Dr. Elisabeth Kübler-Ross's writings that taught me most about death and dying. If death is not sudden, Dr. Kübler-Ross believed that a dying patient upon receiving the diagnosis of a terminal illness would progress through five emotional or psychological stages: denial, anger, bargaining, depression, and acceptance.

In her writings, Dr. Kübler-Ross's patients did not all heal in a physical sense—most didn't—but she would say that they all got better in an emotional or spiritual sense. To heal spiritually did not imply that people were meant to live on earth permanently. To heal spiritually entailed living in the moment, being present, accepting what life offered. To heal spiritually implied preparation for higher experiences in this world or the next.

Naturally, I wanted my mother to recover, but given the dire circumstances, I wanted my mother to at least be spiritually healthy, to be at peace with her own self.

Mother was eventually released from the hospital. She was in great physical discomfort and was suffering from acute anxiety. My brother and I fell into our respective roles: Hayden moved into the house with her and became her primary caretaker attending to her physical needs, and I would attempt to address her emotional needs. This experience brought out the best in Hayden: caring for our mother brought a sense of peace and happiness to his soul.

I simply wanted to provide Mother the opportunity to share, to be a catalyst that might help her to work through her fears and any repressed feelings. There would be lots of challenges for both Hayden and me in our new roles.

For Mother, denial was her purgatory: a state that permitted her fear of dying to be repressed, placed on the back burner, set aside to simmer like her tea upon the stove; I hoped that it could not last forever. When denial was no longer feasible, it was replaced by anger. Then she would openly question, "Why me?" Yet an intense and passionate desire to maintain the will to live endured. She simply wanted to breathe. It was a wonderful gift to leave her children.

Cheryl was one person who could relate to Mother's anguish and anger, for at the age of thirty, she had been diagnosed with breast cancer. She was among the youngest at that time to have been diagnosed on the Island.

The three of us—Cheryl, Mother, and I—were gathered in the hallway of my childhood home. This particular evening, Mother was in a terribly agitated state, the worst I had witnessed yet. In a state of complete exasperation, Mother had begun to physically move away from us and was heading up the stairs. Cheryl could easily sense both Mother's and my depth of frustration.

Cheryl lightly grabbed my forearm, and whispered in my ear, "Do you mind if I speak to your mother alone?"

I shook my head.

"Etta, can I speak with you?"

Mother simply collapsed on the staircase and sat with her head in her hands, a testimony of her despair. Cheryl sat down beside her on the steps. Feeling quite useless, I turned away and left them to their own, closing the hallway door behind me.

After they spoke, Mother was much more at peace with the world. The three of us chatted briefly in the living room. Mother still went to bed early that evening but clearly in a different state of mind. If asked, I could not say that she was happy, but something had changed. There was a sense of resolution. She was quiet, but not angry or depressed.

"What did you talk about?" I asked Cheryl.

"I shared my memories of chemo with her."

"How did it go?"

"I believe the timing was right. Your mom is very angry. She related well when I told how I felt my body betrayed me. She feels betrayed, too."

A few nights later, as Cheryl and I sat around her kitchen table, she went on in greater detail to explain her recent conversation with my mother.

"Two things come to mind when I think of chemotherapy. One is the pre-nauseous state. I'd get so sick on the mornings of the chemo just knowing how sick it was going to make me. The hospital laundry room was down the hall from where I received my treatments. To this day," she said, "the smell of a major laundry can make me sick to my stomach.

"The other memory is of how angry I was at my body. I felt my body betrayed me. I would have given anything for another."

Cheryl poured hot tea into our mugs. In my mind, I tried to apply Cheryl's wisdom to Mother's situation. I thought Cheryl was finished on the subject, but she spoke again.

"It was the first time I was aware that we are so much more than a body."

This moment confirmed what I already knew and always wanted to believe. We are indeed spiritual beings first. We are so much more than a body.

I wanted Mother to embrace the power of positive thinking. I believed that Cheryl's experience would help, so I shared the following the story with Mother.

It took place during the time Cheryl was receiving chemotherapy. As the story goes, Cheryl had gone into the hospital on the morning of one of her initial treatments. Other patients had assembled in this waiting area as well. Eventually, Cheryl's name was called, and she proceeded towards the same day treatment area. This was in the days before the Island's QEH had its cancer wing.

After the treatment, Cheryl was making her way back through the corridors, and, as she entered a glassed-in section of the building, she happened to cross paths with an older woman being accompanied by a nurse. The sun was shining through the windows on that particular morning; Cheryl recalls feeling the sun on her face and enjoying nature's natural warmth. She smiled at the patient and nurse as the two parties neared one another, wished them good morning, and then continued on her way.

On the day of her ensuing treatment, Cheryl happened to run into the same nurse.

"Do you remember us meeting in the glassed walkway last week? I was walking with an elderly lady," the nurse asked.

"Yes, I do."

"The lady who I was walking with had also been recently diagnosed with breast cancer, and, in fact, that morning she was heading for the exact same treatment that you had just finished. We were both impressed with your positive attitude and cheerful disposition. Just after you passed, my patient turned to me and said, 'I wish I had whatever that young lady has.'"

Cheryl was rather taken aback by the story. The nurse noticed Cheryl's reaction and proceeded to explain.

"I believe in the power of positive thinking. I have been nursing for years and have witnessed far too many examples of its value for it to be ignored or overlooked. You definitely have the right attitude to face your illness and recovery."

I shared with Mother that I, too, was a firm believer in the power of positive thinking. Our thoughts influence our health, our actions, and our behaviours, and many other aspects of our future. While she may have strongly desired to breathe, I was concerned with her "dominating fighting spirit"—she never lived in the moment. Mother showed little interest in what previously had seemed to provide meaning and joy in her life. She was obsessed with fighting her illness. Her body was constantly in fight-or-flight mode; it knew no rest.

Mother was always one for routines: she'd do her wash on Mondays; Tuesday was always set aside for baking bread. She made the best homemade bread and would end up giving loaves of it away as little personal gifts.

One morning, Hayden called me at work. He was at the end of his rope. Mother had been advised to rest. Yet, unbeknownst to Hayden, her primary caretaker, she had gotten up earlier than usual that Tuesday morning and had set bread. Knowing that Hayden would have protested, Mother had done this behind his back. With the task completed, she was absolutely exhausted. As a result, she lacked the energy to even get out of bed and had hardly eaten all day. Hayden was now feeling somewhat responsible.

I came out to visit that evening.

"She's still in bed" was the only greeting I received. Hayden was still not at his best. I knew that he hadn't liked being lied to, but, even more importantly, he was concerned that Mother may have harmed herself under his watch.

I proceeded upstairs and found Mother resting in her bed. She looked worn and tired. She knew damn well why I was there.

"You might as well say it as think it," Mother said.

"Well, I was wondering if you were trying to kill yourself. You were told you needed to rest. What were you thinking?"

"I can't lie in this bed and do nothing except get up to go downstairs and watch television. You don't know what it's like. There are some afternoons when I am forced to go to bed, that I literally want to rip my pillow cases and bed sheets to shreds." She put her hands before me showing me the motion, as if it would have been as easy as ripping paper.

Her words were true: I had no idea what it was like.

"I need to bake bread for as long as I can—baking bread to me is what writing is for you."

Baking bread had given her a sense of purpose, a reason to get up that morning.

"I understand that part, Mom. I truly do. We'll work something out, but you can't lie to Hayden or go behind his back. That's not fair."

It made me think of earlier times, when Father had cancer, and I had taken him to walk at the shore, much to my mother's protest. That day she was so worried that something might happen to Father, that he didn't have the energy for the outing. She wanted only to keep her husband home and safe. Funny how perceptions can change, depending on the angle you are looking from.

"Thanks," Mother said. "Now I really do need to rest."

I gave her a kiss on the forehead and headed out of the room. I paused for a moment at the doorway. I had to ask.

"Was it worth it?"

"Definitely."

This comparison of Mother's bread baking to my writing was significant to me; however, initially, it brought forth a rather uncomfortable memory.

The memory that came to mind occurred during the period of time when I had finished my Arts degree, had returned from travelling about Europe, and was back living at home. On this particular day, Mother was doing some preparations in the kitchen, while I was sitting in the living room, writing. Mother came into the room with a dishcloth in her hand. She had an agitated look about her, and she started at me right away.

"I think that you need to make better use of your time."

I put my pen down. "And what would that be?"

"You need to be thinking of getting a trade."

"A trade."

"Yes, a trade—become a carpenter or a plumber, something that will earn you some money."

"I have no interest in learning a trade. Besides, I like to write."

"Writing is not a job. You have to earn a living."

"I'm going to return to university in the fall, Mom. Not everyone has to do a trade. Just because your family did, doesn't mean that I have to. That's not who I am."

"Well, you can't just stay inside and write something for others to read."

"You and Hayden spend hours watching television. What's the difference?"

For a few unspoken minutes, Mother stood in the archway that connected both rooms, before walking away. I could tell she was frustrated with how our conversation had gone. She was growing frustrated with me. I guess we were growing frustrated with each other.

That incident with my mother had more impact on me than I realized at the time. It was a defining moment in our relationship which would take years to unpack. This verbal exchange certainly did not encourage my interest in writing; in fact, the argument did not encourage me to be me. I was struggling to be who I was— or who I AM. I allowed my mother's lack of support to become a barrier in my own development. She did not encourage my psychic interests or my love of literature and writing: two primary interests that helped define me. I was normal in my development—

I wanted my mother to be supportive of who I was, not who she wanted me to be.

We never spoke of my writing again, and I thought she might have forgotten the incident… until the bread-baking event.

On that afternoon, while my mom lay exhausted in bed from baking bread, she was giving me messages well beyond her acceptance of my writing: one, she was modelling to me the necessity of having a sense of purpose and meaning in your life regardless of how dire your situation is. She was revealing the need to get beyond your illness. Two, she proved to me that she understood me far better than she ever let on. And, three, she was demonstrating that people could change.

Mother's beliefs began to change after she took sick. It was like she had truly begun to look at who she was and had given herself permission to question and to acknowledge that some of her old beliefs were no longer working. She would gradually expand this process to more and more beliefs, eventually questioning her upbringing, religion, and purpose in life. While it was unfortunate that Mother had to wait until she took sick before challenging some of her beliefs, it was still a beautiful process to witness.

At the time, I also found it rather interesting that Mother compared her bread baking to my writing and not to my work. She now knew what things in life truly mattered. It was like she had come home to herself. It was a yet another great teaching to leave us with.

Around this time I began to reflect more and more on one of life's greatest spiritual truths: free will. And it was a difficult concept to comprehend. Not everyone is comfortable with the idea of free will. And there are varying interpretations.

I came to believe that much of the purpose of this life was to experience many and varied aspects of it, and the significance of these experiences was to learn lessons. It wasn't that the experiences in and of themselves were everything; equally important was how we reacted to these experiences—what we decided to do with our lives as a result of having lived these experiences. It was these personal choices that would determine who we are and who we will become.

As humans, we are all blessed with the ability to consciously reflect, to be rational and reflect on our experiences. Then we can transcend our circumstances. But we can't reflect unless we are open to receive these teachings, these lessons. First and foremost, we have to become aware. As humans, we have been given free will to accept these teachings or to ignore them.

What I struggled with was the concept of our lives being predetermined. I had been raised in the traditions of the Catholic Church, which teaches predestation as part of their doctrine; however, I could not believe that people would be predestined to be tortured or raped. I could not accept that God/Spirit had predetermined anyone to be evil. My God/Spirit was a God/Spirit of love and grace.

But I loved how the American clairvoyant, Edgar Cayce, saw the world, thinking that we are predetermined to the extent that our past thinking and experiences limit us in probability and incline us in a certain direction, but—and it is a big but—"free will can always draw the sword from the stone." Thus he believed both free will and predestination coexist in a person.

If we are predetermined, I believe it is solely with the purpose to become whole, to find God/Spirit's grace, to express our divinity. This is a universal force: from whole to holy. Life will push us towards experiences to heal our souls if we make ourselves available. We all may seek unique, individual paths—that's our free will—but we all start out from the same place and have an innate desire to return to that original source. It is our divine nature. We are predetermined to manifest God/Spirit's grace. In essence, we are all pilgrims on an inner journey to our holy place.

And we meet this desire by self-actualizing, by finding meaning and purpose in our lives, by serving others, by belonging to one another—all of this is interwoven to draw us into a closer communication with God/Spirit.

At any time, with sincere effort and determination, we can change.

We can overcome addictions.

We can ask for help.

We can practice mindfulness.

We can change who we are.

We don't have to change all of our beliefs; we simply need to be healthy and mature enough to investigate our beliefs—and be willing to discard what no longer is working for us.

I do not believe Divine Intervention would ever give us the answers to all of life's most important questions when it is our responsibility to learn, to discover, to make use of our free will. How else could anyone spiritually evolve?

In my own life situation, I struggled, for I, too, had a choice. I could choose to respond in forgiveness, openness, and love as readily as choosing to respond in anger or fear. I could choose to treat my spiritual experiences as gifts or a blessing, or continue to view them as private acts to be hidden from the scrutiny or judgement of others. I could choose to learn that all of life's lessons were opportunities to grow and come to accept that lessons in love are not always positive and beautiful on the surface.

The truth: I was still making spiritual choices based on fear.

My shorefront walks continued, but now, at least in the physical sense, I was alone. These walks eventually became practices of prayer and confession, as I would walk the shorefront purging my soul to God/Spirit and the sea. In my despair, I clung to my relationship with my Creator, for it gave me great comfort in a time of unknown.

Mother was not the only one who went through the stages of grief. At the height of her illness, I felt as if I was going through stages of adjustment similar to Mother, only at a much lower, less intense level. On one shore walk I literally roared at the ocean, "Why the hell do I have to lose both parents when most people my age haven't lost one?" My anger was a perfect distraction for what was truly upsetting me: my mother was dying, and I did not want to accept that.

On other walks, I would bargain, pray, and then bargain again. On other days these conversations would take on a different flow as I asked for acceptance. Then one day I openly acknowledged: "I continue to pray to you, but I'm not sure that I any longer believe in you."

Like any relationship, my bond with God/Spirit was being tested.

And there it was, another lesson that I would eventually come to learn. Prayer was being truthful with God/Spirit. If I was going to have an authentic relationship with God/Spirit, then I had to be truthful. The truth had to be more significant than success, image, popularity, or acceptance. I had to strive to be truthful with God/Spirit, which meant being honest and real with everyone—which meant beginning by being honest with myself.

In *Help Thanks Wow*, Anne Lamott shares her belief that when a person is telling the truth, she or he is most close to God. She writes, "So prayer is our sometimes real selves trying to communicate with the Real, with Truth, with the Light." Even when we hate God, she believes that state is prayer as well because we are being real, "and maybe it is the first sincere thought you've had in months." The point is that like Lamott, I believe God can handle honesty; and what is true prayer but honest, open conversation, our authentic selves communicating with the Truth?

As a child, God/Spirit spoke to me and encouraged me to question, to never live in a lie.

So why wouldn't I also question her/him if that's what it takes to get to the truth?

Then s/he would at least know my search was sincere.

The presence of a priest caught me unexpectedly. A friend and I had been attending a talk at a church hall, and, during intermission, I took a leisurely stroll alongside the neighbouring graveyard while waiting for my friend to come and join me. The priest recognized me, walked over, and started a conversation. Eventually, he asked about the well-being of a former colleague of mine whom he happened to know well enough through his former parish.

"The talk is that her mother is not doing well," the priest uttered.

"No, Father, that's very true. Her mother is quite ill."

"Your friend will take that hard, won't she?" As he spoke, he nodded his head in self-agreement. I was uncertain as to whether this man was alluding to the severity of grief generally associated with the death of one's parent, or if he simply was acknowledging the gentle, compassionate nature of my former colleague. I offered him my silence to allow him to elaborate if he so wished, and he did.

"It amazes me how this grieving can drag on for such lengths for some people. You must see this type of thing quite often in your line of work."

I was lost for words, but it mattered little for before I could collect my thoughts and share how greatly I am often touched by grief and bereavement in both my work and private life, this man, fixed on his original point, interrupted me and continued on with the sound of his own voice.

"My own mother died. I was lonesome. I missed her presence, but I carried on. Some of these people allow themselves to fall apart." He fluttered his hand in midair. "It becomes all emotion." He took a deep breath that bordered on a sigh. Then his tone became more serious, more concentrated. "I find this very draining. It can be very tiring to deal with."

I held my tongue. My words and beliefs were not going to change this man. Besides, he was entitled to his opinion. I simply did not see bereavement through his eyes.

"I guess that's the beauty of human nature, Father, we're all different." Then I added, "Thank God."

"Yes, I guess that you are right," he concluded. Then he clasped his hands behind his back, turned unassumingly, and walked away.

We are all different. We do not all love the same. Unless you have willingly exposed your soul to the utmost depths of your pain and loss, you can't possibly lead another through their uncharted waters.

My friend returned to join me shortly after the priest and I had parted ways. I was quite content to take leave of his company and to continue my walk along those hallowed lands, knowing as Tolstoy did that loving strongly can cause a person to suffer great sorrow but that very same love will someday counteract your grief and heal you.

Christian mystic Edgar Cayce once said, "Pay more attention to your dreams, for this is where truths are given." Since receiving the communication in Guyana, I had become more conscious of my dreams. Many were very intense, so I began to record a number of them in a journal.

The following dream took place shortly after Mother had completed her first round of treatments:

Saturday, May 3, 1997
South Rustico

Last night I had a dream. In my dream, I dreamt that Mother had a dream. She had come to me, so that I might help interpret it for her.

In my mother's dream, her house was on fire.

Upon hearing her words, I immediately comprehended her dream as symbolizing that Mother's cancer had returned. Her home was her body, and the fire was the cancer spreading, burning in the ovarian cavity of her body. I was jolted from my sleep in the same state that only seconds before I had heard the image of my mother describe. For in my dream, my mother talked of waking from her sleep feeling terror that so much was being lost.

In a matter of days, Mother's test results would indicate that the treatment intervention had not been successful. The cancer had not been beaten. It had in fact returned with a vengeance. A new, stronger treatment was being considered. The doctors now began to speak in terms of remission as opposed to cure.

Spiritual dreams can be overwhelming. It has been said that symbolism is the language of the unconscious mind. Much of society was not ready to accept or at least to acknowledge the validity of premonitions and spiritual insights, not ready to accept any information other than rational, analytical thought. I knew enough that I had to be open and ready for any spiritual experience to believe in them. I was not willing to ignore the messages in my dreams.

Eventually, the topic of organized religion arose.

One evening during the early stages of Mother's relapse, I listened outside her bedroom door. Her voice was weak and strained as she rattled off a litany of petitionary prayers. She was rushing her words, as if forced or compelled to do so. This lady, who had been so passionate about religion, had now become obsessed with praying: praying for her own well-being and the souls of others. I opened her bedroom door, for I could not stand to listen unbeknownst to her any longer. She was in such a wretched state. Her tiny hands were caressing the blessed beads of her rosary, her gaunt fingers jumping from one red bead to the next. The recent months of illness were etched upon her face. Her throat had grown thin, and her eyes appeared to have set back into their frame. The praying obsession had been going on for days. As I drew near her, she was praying in such a fury that her words were barely decipherable to my ears. My presence did little to thwart her compulsion. Her childlike eyes glanced up at me, requesting patience and understanding for this ritual that had to be completed. So I waited. How I longed to take the flowing rosary from her frantic hands and calm her quivering lips. Instead, I just sat with her.

A few weeks later, I felt Mother was in a different place emotionally, and I felt comfortable enough to discuss her recent obsession with the rosary.

"I feel like I'm losing my religion, my connection with God," Mother said.

"Can you forgive God for allowing your cancer?" I asked.

"I don't blame God... anymore."

"Why were you praying so?"

"I was praying because I literally feared I might drop dead if I ever stopped, even for a moment. I can see it now. I couldn't then. I know that I was being irrational. I guess you would refer to it as more of my 'self-denial.' Is that the term you use?"

I ignored that question. "Are you questioning your faith?"

"Do you know that I have never felt able to? Never. I didn't believe that I could. Didn't believe that I was even allowed. Isn't that foolish!" She slapped her hands upon her knees so hard that the motion drew her head and shoulders forward.

The recent weeks had brought about a change in Mother, a change beyond the physical. She now desired to speak with me in private, and she looked forward to our time alone. We would sit, and she would speak openly, and for the most part, I would listen.

"I really thought I was losing my mind for a while. By times, I would be so angry. The next, I would feel so helpless or even feel sorry for myself. Then, before I knew it, I'd be angry again." Her hands rose in the air registering her frustration and confusion.

"Don't anyone ever come in and tell me this is God's will for me. Don't anybody dare."

The roots of her anger had finally surfaced.

The topic of her obsessive praying would come up time and time again, and she openly shared how her behaviour eventually came to frighten her. She would speak of denial and come once again to the subject of religion, a theme that had obviously been festering for a time.

"When I was growing up, they did not allow us to question our faith, let alone encourage us to question the ways of the church.

We were not like the young people of today. We were taught to simply accept the teachings."

"Who are *they*, Mother?" I asked.

"The priests and the nuns. My parents. Teachers. Most adults that I would have come in contact with. I doubt if they all believed the same, but that was how it felt to me. When I was young."

"How does it feel to question now?"

"I'm still not sure. You'd think I'd know by now. I don't think anyone was doing any wrong. Intentionally wrong. But that still doesn't make it right, does it? What do you think?"

"I think that it's always good to question, Mom. Always."

Time began to feel extra precious; it seemed even more vital to make the most of every day. Mother and I had grown even closer since the death of my father. As her health deteriorated, she became even more open and in addition to her views on religion, she began to disclose more and more details about her troubled childhood and young adulthood years and perspectives on life in general.

Through the course of a few similar conversations, it became clear to me that my mother did not blame the church, the nuns, and/or the priests. She understood. In her eyes, these people had only accepted the moral, religious, and dogmatic teachings that had been current for hundreds of years and had been passed down to them. But she could now accept that much of the dogma had lost its original function and no longer served people well. She was an adult nearing sixty, living with terminal cancer before she ever took time to reflect and consider the true nature of her beliefs. Had she not developed cancer, she may have been content to continue to live out her life in a similarly submissive manner.

I could not help but think how different her life might have been had she not felt such bondage and had questioned. How my life, and that of my brother, would be different as well. I felt blessed to have been encouraged to question—first by my childhood message and now by my dying mother, regardless of how late in her life it may have been. I felt it was now my responsibility to eventually pass this gift onto others.

In many ways, I was childlike again, but in a good way.

While I struggled emotionally to come to terms with my father's secret sexuality and family betrayal, the protection of my mother, and the consuming responsibilities of my mother's health, I became equally enthralled with the enriching beauty that I found surrounding me. I was filled with a sense of wonder; I was finding simple pleasures in the varying aspects of the day-to-day world. In my free time, I was still seeking answers, but I was just as determined to enjoy as many moments of life along the way.

It was a healthy childishness, a dichotomous concept. I felt that I had been offered a glimpse into a richer, more evolved awareness of this world; I felt an inspiring sense of obligation to appreciate what this world truly offers. In many ways, it was an overwhelming sense of gratitude. In the years that followed, as I came to know myself better, as I came to terms with the crisis and conflicts in my life, as I became more unified as a person, this sense of reverence for life only continued to grow and grow.

As a direct result of these unexplained spiritual experiences, I was convinced that life would only continue to get better, in a richer and more meaningful way. It would simply take time, patience, and trust. This thinking was a gift in itself.

It was all about the statue.

It would have been Monday, September 8, the day the Catholic Church recognizes as the Nativity of the Blessed Mother. Mother was resting in bed, but she looked vigorous, not at all what I had been expecting. She had called me at work, which she rarely did, and had asked me to come out that evening for a visit. When I entered her bedroom, she was all business and immediately motioned me to take a seat in the familiar well-worn rocking chair, a baby shower gift to acknowledge my arrival into this world thirty-six years prior.

"I need to share with you something that occurred last night."

There was no small talk as Mother led instantly into her story.

"I had gone to bed around nine. I was resting, facing the wall," Mother extended her right arm and touched the neighbouring wall, "when I was disturbed from my rest by a voice." She looked directly at me, as if questioning me before she even shared her story. "The voice was coming from within my room. I was sure I was alone, so I questioned aloud who was there." She paused her storyline. "I wasn't asleep." Her voice rose slightly to stress the point. "It took me a while to realize that the voice I was hearing was coming from the direction of my statue of St. Teresa," and with her left hand, Mother extended her index finger and pointed diagonally to the corner behind me.

For the life of me, I did not dare move my head, for I knew exactly what she was referring to: a statue of St. Teresa, Mother's patron saint, had been a permanent resident in recent years within the confines of Mother's bedroom. The statue, dressed in a cloak of white, hands united in prayer, the base cracked, and in various sections such as the clasped hands, chin, and bare feet, the paint was chipped. The statue adorned a small linen-covered table in the corner of the room directly behind me.

"The voice questioned, 'Etta, why do you want to live?' and I answered, aloud, 'I want to get better and help others and be with my boys.'"

Mother was not merely retelling her story, but, on some level, I believe she was reliving the experience. Her eyes looked beyond me at the statue in question. Her look was intense and trusting. Then she jolted back to the present, and her gaze returned to me.

"I didn't hesitate to reply. I wasn't the least bit nervous, and I spoke out loud, not feeling the least out of place."

Mother spoke calmly; her tone was void of fervour or anxiousness. I searched for traces of fantasy but could find none. She continued, "What stands out most was the calmness and peacefulness of the voice and the absolute lack of fear I felt." Then: "Do you believe me?"

I was lost for words. I had no idea if Mother had once again regressed to a state of denial. My fingers gripped the wooden ends of the rocking chair's protruding arms, and the rounded strips of wood pressed upon my back. I sat there trying to picture myself telling people, *In the fall of '97, the statue of St. Teresa spoke to my dying mother. Yes, the miracle of Oyster Bed Bridge, the speaking statue, took place in the privacy of her bedroom where just over a month previously the beloved was confessing of her desire to rip her bed to shreds.*

What a hypocrite I was. I wanted to believe her. Who was I to say that she couldn't have experienced a miracle? Who was I to challenge the validity of anyone else's experiences? It was only a little more than a year ago, in Guyana, that I wrote in my own handwriting of receiving a message. Who was I to say that her message was any less real? I had been in my mother's shoes, though I lacked her fortitude. I didn't speak of my own spiritual experiences. I was still being critical and sceptical. Had I not learned anything? I wanted to believe my mother, but I just couldn't allow myself that gift. I refused to show my doubt, so I faked it.

"If you say it's so, then I believe you, Mom," I finally answered.

The truth was, I believed that the experience was real to her.

This single event manifested an overwhelming sense of calmness within Mother in the days that immediately followed. I would watch her face light up with each account she selectively shared. It was a new beginning in this journey; I believe Mother for once had given up fighting her cancer and had placed her energy on living. She had transcended the battle and had not conceded; she was now approaching the fight from a different perspective. It was like the healing had begun.

Like I had done with my own experiences, Mother elected not to share with others, with the exception of myself. The experience was real to her and that seemed to be enough. Though most were unaware of her recent experience, everyone who came in contact with her during that time acknowledged the apparent change in Mother for there was a marked difference in her attitude.

"She is doing so much better," people would say, or "Aren't your mother's spirits great these days."

In the days that followed, no further talk of the voice transpired between Mother and me, and I had no desire to bring up the issue, to disturb the harmony. I think we both needed a few days to absorb the event and to comprehend its relevance. Though, intrinsically, I direly wanted to know Mother's interpretation of the event.

After a period of time had passed, I eventually approached the subject with her.

"You're more relaxed, Mother. You're not fighting so much, if you know what I mean."

"I am more relaxed," Mother assured me. "I was too busy praying to be healed. Pleading to God, telling Him how to do His job... I was consumed. I know we spoke of this before, but I had allowed my praying to become an obsession."

"Mother, I'd say it was more like a penance."

She ignored my comment.

"Now I only pray when I like. And my prayers bring me joy again." Mother was trying to live her faith as opposed to forcing it.

"And all of this because of hearing a voice?"

Mother simply nodded her head in agreement. "St. Teresa's voice," she clarified.

"What do you think that all really means, Mom? The voice. Coming from a statue."

And that is the point in the conversation where I wished I had stopped. There are several moments in my life where I have questioned, in hindsight, how I dealt with a situation, and none more so than this particular situation involving my mother.

Mother responded immediately. "I see it as a sign of recovery… I have absolutely no fear or apprehension of the upcoming treatments, though I know I can expect to be deathly ill as a result of them. I feel a sense of security in light of my recent experience. I know I will be able to withstand my upcoming chemo."

This was where we had differed. It was the idea of healing making you whole—that's what I was looking so intently for in my mother: a sense of peace and spiritual comfort. I had supposed that the voice, the sense of security, and the ensuing peacefulness that she experienced in the face of death spoke to Mother of life after death, proof of God/Spirit or some greater force. I believed the serenity attributed to the voice would have relieved her fears of dying, which would help her live. That she might heal. That it might also be interpreted as a sign of life for those who had gone before her and of the new life that might await her; however, for Mother, it instilled hope, but only hope on this side of the border.

Still, I moved forward.

"Mom, has the thought ever occurred to you that the voice might have wished to grant you peace, to ease your fight with death?

Maybe the voice was questioning why you deny its very existence. I am by no means implying that death is close. I just wonder if this voice was so spiritual, so meaningful, could it not offer peace in that way? Could it not mean that there is some degree of serenity that awaits us all?"

I needed to ask.

"Mother, I need to know what you think. Many who have gone before you would have welcomed this newfound peace, this sign of something more. Could it not mean both peace for today and peace after death?"

"I honestly never thought of it in that manner." That was all she said.

Mother wasn't interested in what others had to say about her spiritual experience, not even her son in whom she had confided. She wanted to be her own expert witness and was not ready for me or for anyone else to try to interpret her private experience. Her own personal interpretation or reflection was enough. I had no intent of denouncing the validity of her premonition or questioning her personal "expert witness" interpretation of the event; I simply wanted to understand both the event and my mother. I certainly did not wish to take from Mother any sense of hope.

Our conversation just ended. Unsure of what to say, I simply smiled and rose from my childhood rocking chair and went over to hug my ailing mother. That was enough discussion for one night. She went to sleep with a smile on her face and her precious statue overlooking her in the corner. There was a sense of contentment about her.

The following night, Cheryl and I took Moody Dog, who was but a pup, out for a visit. Mom was enthralled watching the puppy running and tripping across the living room. My godmother, Mom's sister, was visiting from Ontario, and another sister was there as well. It was a beautiful gathering, and we all made the most of the evening. There was clearly a sense of peace about Mother that we all hadn't seen in ages, as she absorbed everyone's love. Regardless of her physical condition, maybe parts of her had truly begun to heal.

Within a month, Mother's health significantly worsened. She didn't break down, she didn't get angry, and she didn't lament whatever voice had led her to believe that she was cured. The sickness associated with the treatments got so intense Mother was unsure whether she could physically withstand the pain and discomfort. She began to question whether she could even continue with the treatments. There was no talk of the statue, at least in my presence, ever again.

Mother never was cured, but I believe she healed. She became whole.

The following four stories occurred during this period of time when my mother's cancer had returned and she eventually returned to the hospital. The doctors had increased the dosage of her treatments, and Mother was desperately sick. They had also determined that additional surgery might be required if she had any hope of prolonging her life. There were two questions that had to be answered: one, if her days were limited, was it worth it to live them in a state of such sickness, and two, was she strong enough to even survive the operation?

I share these brief narratives for they cover the full range of emotions that we were both enduring. It would be deceitful of me to portray myself as living in a state of bliss and control, as if I was merely sitting around writing reflective journal entries and reading thoughtful, related literature, mindfully pondering on spirituality. Life, I assure you, was far more complicated and was being lived.

1. The Haircut

Soon her hair began to fall from her scalp in larger clumps. Hayden shared with me that when she awoke in the mornings, Mother tried her best to rid her pillowcase and bedsheets of the strands of miscellaneous hair before anyone might enter her room and view the mess. She absolutely abhorred those loose clumps of hair, those constant reminders of her despairing health. To add further insult, with the increased loss of hair, now her wig fit even worse. One night, I took the liberty of arriving in Oyster Bed Bridge with a borrowed pair of clippers, hair scissors, and a barber's cape. I was going to offer to shave her head in the privacy of her home.

"You're serious!" was all she said when she saw me standing idly in the hallway with my instruments in hand.

"Yes, I am."

"Can you do it? Can you really cut hair?"

"It's not like I'm going to style it, Mother."

As though she was fearful that she'd change her mind if she delayed for even a minute, Mother threw off the afghan that had been wrapped about her and headed directly to the kitchen sink. She ran warm water over her scalp, but she lacked the energy to even raise her arms long enough to wash her thinning hair. I grabbed the bottle of shampoo that had appeared out of nowhere and squirted a dab onto her head. There was so little hair and her head felt so small in my hands. Then I gently towelled her head and led her to a waiting kitchen chair. As I tied the plastic cape about her neck, few words were exchanged between us. She sat quietly with her hands folded as if in prayer. I remember that I could hear the television set in the adjoining room. A hockey game was being played. It was as if neither of us knew how to response to this situation, to the matter of a simple haircut.

Small clumps of hair began to fall about her feet. Mother brushed away the loose hairs that had drifted aimlessly upon her lap. Having done as much damage as I could with the scissors, I plugged in the razor. Below me, my mother, who had still not said a word, was quietly weeping.

"You okay, Mom?" I whispered.

"I'm all right."

Mother took a moment to wipe her checks. I didn't dare speak. Because of her tears, now there was some of my own welling in my eyes.

In her soft voice, Mother eventually broke her silence. "I am very pleased to have seen other ladies with their heads shaven," her hands lapping softly on her thighs. "Before that, I totally associated feminine baldness with death."

"You're going to look beautiful, Mom. Trust me. Absolutely beautiful."

On a Thursday night, in the privacy of my childhood home, a hockey game playing in the background, my brother's presence bringing a sense of comfort, I felt so connected to my mother as I shaved her head, her hair falling silently to the floor. The act felt so spiritual, so meaningful. I would find it difficult in the coming days to recapture this essence.

2. The Journal Entry

November 2, 1997

It is a hard image to get used to. One I may never become accustomed to. One I hope I will not be forced to become immune to. The image I speak of is that of viewing my mother sitting on the bathroom floor, her body frail and feeble, and she requesting water. She has vomited yet again. In her need for independence she had wandered to the washroom alone. She is so weak that it takes all of her energy, her control, to merely perform this bodily function. Sitting on the cool tiled floor, her shaved head resting on her arm, which is resting on the porcelain rim.

I help Mother clean herself. We talk as I wipe her face with a freshly dampened facecloth. She takes the glass of water that I offer and rinses her mouth. Outside, it is raining hard. "Can you hear the rain, Mother?" She passes back the glass and assures me we need the rain. Weather was always a preoccupation with her…country living.

I see that she gets back into bed and watch as she pulls the covers up close and about her neck before I return downstairs to the kitchen and the morning dishes, a routine endlessly endured by my caring brother. It is Sunday morning. I read some sections from Living Buddha, Living Christ *by Thich Nhat Hanh and a few pages from Ken Wilber's* Eye to Eye.

As for my own mental state, I'm more at peace today— acceptance, though I know this will fluctuate. Things will get worse as time progresses. Just yesterday, I described myself to a friend as an animal about to face a winter and instead of food I am storing peace, rest, and energy for all that may lie ahead.

3. The Curse of Being Human

There was little left to the imagination. It embarrasses me to write this, but I had grown so tired of the sickness. I abhorred the cursed smell of sickness and watching her day to day getting worse. It was difficult to find meaning in her suffering. I recall it was another Saturday night. I had made a point of relieving Hayden most

Saturday nights, taking my turn, so to speak, so that he could get a well-needed physical and mental break. In truth, I wanted to be with Cheryl, but I had nothing to give. Mother was nestled into the oversized armchair; I told myself that I was pleased that for once she was not sprawled over the couch. Mother could sense my frustration that evening but said nothing. She just watched as I unfolded my sleeping bag, spreading the edges out upon the living room floor, and then kneeling to place my pillows. Finally, she spoke.

"Do you know what I've been thinking of, love?"

"No, Mother, I haven't a clue."

"I'd love to go camping this summer."

I lost it.

"Mother, you haven't camped in twenty-some years, and you hated it then."

I remained on my knees, smoothing out my bedding, but my heart was pounding. I could not for the life of me let it go. I stood but did not face her, but my words became more pronounced and clearer.

"You… have… cancer. You, Mother, are wasting away to nothing … before my very eyes… vomiting each bloody morning and most days, and all you wish to talk about is going camping." The single word, *camping*, hung like a curse through the living room air. "Just because you deny it, doesn't make it any less fucking real." I grabbed my bedding and hurled it into the corner of the room and watched a plant fall in its wake. It was the accumulation of her denial, my fatigue, my unspoken resentment, the pain of witnessing her demise.

I was not mature enough to question, why wouldn't she want to go camping? To have some quality of life outside of these damn walls and off of that cursed couch? I fell back to my knees. Mother remained where she was, sitting quietly behind me. Her only response was not to respond. That said it all.

A little voice in my head reminded me that this could be my final coherent conversation with my mother. I wanted to look at her. I wanted to say, "I don't blame you for dying; you didn't will this." I wanted to say, "I don't blame the medical world for failing to extend your life." I especially wanted to say, "I'm sorry," but I, too, said nothing, and she passed by me on her way to bed, and no one even said, "Goodnight."

And she with only months to live.

4. A Lesson from Loneliness

In the fall of Mother's final year, as each passing treatment showed little signs of improvement, her spirits began to waver.

"I'm lonely," Mother confined to Hayden and myself.

"Mom, people are lonely in many ways. What does loneliness mean to you?" I asked.

"I miss going out," she explained. "I miss the simple pleasure of attending various functions and visiting friends. I'm saddened, not envious, of other couples going so freely to different places. It really feels like that old saying of being alone in a crowd. Increasing visitors or having more friends drop in does not fix the situation. I need people who can relate, but I don't believe I'm ready for those support groups you've talked about." Her hands twitched and she wrung them lightly.

"Is there anything else that you're not saying?"

"I have lived"—Mother paused, looking for the right words—"what I perceive as a life of giving, and now I feel so alone. It doesn't seem fair." Her voice cracked.

"Honestly, there are times when I, too, feel disappointed and hurt," I admitted. "Hurt because the lives our own friends and those of the whole community—the community that you gave so much of yourself to so willingly—is carrying on without missing a beat. It pisses me off. It angers me to hear you say you feel so alone, to feel alone after all you have given."

"I don't see it like that." Hayden piped in. "Sorry," he added, sensing my anger. "I'm just not angry at anyone. There were lots of times when other families were in crisis and my world didn't end. I wasn't knocking their door down. Maybe I should have, but I didn't."

"That's you," I argued. "That's not our mother. She went out. She did visit, and where the hell is everyone now?"

"Sure. Mother was there more than I ever was or likely will ever be, but these people probably have other issues in their lives. I'm not making excuses for them. They probably could be more involved. We all could. You're involved more in other people's lives way more than I am because of your line of work. Maybe it hits home more to you than me. I'm just not ready to blame anyone else for something I might not have done either. My only concerns are about our mother, and I don't think any of this talk will help."

Mother smiled at both of us. "Hayden's right, Adrian," she said looking directly at me. "I was quick to judge others. People forget the loneliness. We all do, or else we couldn't move on."

Though the roles were reversed, I was acting like the mother in Jane Urquhart's beautiful historical novel, *The Stone Carvers*, which so eloquently portrays how people deal with lost loved ones. When Helga Becker, the mother of the main characters, cannot deal with the separation from her son, Urquhart writes, "She seemed to be perpetually angered by the superficiality of a world that could continue on with its business in the face of the total dematerialization of her son." I was stuck there, too.

I should have simply listened. Mother had a right to feel bitter, even if only briefly. By reacting like I did, I made the issue bigger then it was—I made it about me. Mother was not dwelling in self-pity—I was. She did not believe that the world owed her anything—I did.

When you are witnessing a loved one dying, sometimes fear comes out as anger. I was wrong to judge. Mother and Hayden had accepted people as they were. They were quick to forgive. They realized that other people had lives to live, which meant they had their own families to attend to, their own challenges and obligations. Mother's friends were real; they had withdrawn to a certain degree—such is life—but they had not abandoned her. In the coming months, they would prove this time and time and time again.

This message recently came back to me while I read *Father Fiction* by Donald Miller. Miller describes God's love as "withdrawal without abandonment." God gives you life, and then he/she stands back so that you can take risks, evolve, and grow, but he/she is there in times of real need. You need to be able to stay connected and start again from where you left off, regardless of the period of time that has expired. But you also need your own space. That's what Mother's friends were truly doing.

Eventually, the family had to accept that Mother was not getting any better and that my brother could no longer continue to be the main caretaker and continue to look after Mother in her own home. There was now talk that the treatments would be discontinued. As a last effort, Mother was going to be hospitalized again, and her medical team was considering the possibility of additional surgery. It became a waiting game. Mother and I continued to have our regular conversations.

"Mom, do you ever think of death?" I asked one night not long before she was hospitalized. She was resting on the couch as I recall.

Mother bent her frail arm and rubbed her thinning fingers along her forehead as she paused to collect her thoughts. "I don't feel that my immediate death is close, if that is what you mean."

I did not respond, and, when I did not answer, she began to speak again.

"I believe that I will actually feel the dawning of my death when the time is near. And that it will be a time of inner peace." Her glance left me briefly to search the surroundings of the room; I watched her hands smooth out the flow of the blanket that she was covered in. "Don't get me wrong. I am not welcoming death. And I just don't believe it is near. I definitely don't fear it in the same light as I have all along."

I believed that the experience with the statue had truly helped.

Silence absorbed both of us. I reflected on Mother's confession in the privacy of my thoughts. Then a smile came to Mother's rather pensive face.

"What are you thinking of?" I questioned.

"I'm thinking of a childhood incident," Mother said, and then she smiled even wider. "It's one that I have seldom shared. But I'll tell you if you like."

"I'd love to hear it."

"I had a childhood friend who lost a sister. Her sister was young and had this terrible illness and was hospitalized coming on the end. We were all children. I went with my friend to visit her sister in the hospital during those last days. It would have been one of the few times I had ever entered the old Charlottetown Hospital as a child. It felt as if a thick veil surrounded everyone within that room"—Mother's right hand swung in a half circle before her, her fingers spreading wide—"keeping the room cold and impersonal. The word 'death' was never so much as uttered by the family. Not that night or on any evening that would follow, at least while I was in their presence. To this day, I will swear on my mother's grave that my dear friend regrets that she never broke her family's silence and spoke openly and honestly, primarily for her dying sister's sake but for her own good, too.

"It could have been a beautiful time for closure and closeness," my mother acknowledged. "Those hanging emotions never went away. I know they never left this grieving family. I was only a child, but I remember thinking that I never ever wanted my family to live like that. Love, I don't wish to die like that either."

"Mom, speaking of death does not imply a lack of hope. Accepting death does not infer wishing death. Accepting death has little to do with dying but a world of meaning to living. Accepting death, I believe, only encourages a person to live a richer, more meaningful life. It's a means to a spiritual appreciation."

With that comment, Mother chuckled. "I remember your own father, my husband, saying very similar words to me a number of years ago." She paused in her thoughts and shook her head from side to side. "You know, I could not accept that belief until I had experienced my own mother's death. Even with the childhood memory that I just shared, I couldn't bring myself to even discuss death. I believed that death did not belong in my world. The talk was too morbid. How foolish this thinking was." And she chuckled once again aloud and at herself.

Mother was hospitalized before the treatments were completed. She was too ill to undergo surgery and too sick to remain at home. The specialists believed that hospice care was now the best option, maybe her only option. I remember well the first conversation I had with Mother after the specialists had made their recommendation.

"Did the nurse mention the hospice to you?" Mother asked, not even allowing me the time to get my coat off. She was sitting up in the hospital bed as if she had been waiting for me.

"Yes, she did, Mom," I answered.

There were tears in her voice, and Mother began to tremble big. "I don't want to go there, Adrian." She paused, but I knew what was coming next. "People go there to die." Tears materialized and streamed down her cheeks. Then her voice softened. "Your dad died there... I'll die there."

Mother believed that the hospice was a death sentence. At the time, I, too, honestly believed that she would die in hospice care, but I'd be damned if I was going to agree with her. There were no words within me that morning that could hold any meaning, but then words are not always necessary. So I simply held this shell of a person.

That night after talking to Mother about the hospice I had a dream. I dreamt there was a small boy being housed in some form of institution, and he desperately wished to leave, of this I was certain. As night approached, the child and another slightly older boy planned to escape. It was winter, and there was a white horse there. There were two men, serving as guards, on watch. One guard was middle-aged and overweight; the other was older and appeared more serious—not angered, just sincere. The two men witnessed the children take flight on the back of the horse. The older and fitter of the two guards gave chase.

In the hope that his pursuer would follow the path of the horse, the young boy, who had been sitting at the rear, jumped from the horse's back, taking leave of his companion. Then quickly he scurried through the thicker foliage of the woods and eventually took cover in the overhang of an evergreen's branches. The tips of the branches weighted with snow nearly touched the hard and frozen ground. The little guy lay there listening and shivering. He could hear his own breath and the beat of his heart. The guard who remained on the rooftop shouted directions from high above, identifying the horse's movements, the more obvious escape route. The boy could hear the man calling out that he could see the tracks the horse had made. The boy smiled to himself but did not dare to move just yet.

Then in my dream all I saw was a single foot.

The older guard had neglected the obvious and, instead, had chosen to walk among the forest. It was as if he had felt the child's presence. Now the child could sense that he had been espied, that all was lost. In despair, he drifted off into a deep sleep, leaving the situation entirely in the hands of this man. It was a state of absolute submission, of vulnerable trust even in the unknown. Then all I could see was the guard's eye, and I was awake.

My eyes opened to the familiarity of my bedroom wall. I felt only the hands of another as someone tucked the top of my comforter in around my exposed and shivering shoulders. "Do not be afraid. I wanted to see that you were comfortable. I love you."

Gradually I gained awareness that I was alone, that my visitor had gone. I felt a great sense of comfort from the visit.

Christmas Day, 1997
Brighton

What I cannot believe in is miracles, martyrs, and Father Christmas. In heaven and hell and angels on clouds and tormented souls. That there is meaning in Mother's suffering.

Original sin. I cannot believe that song and drink and festive merriment will ease my unrelenting loneliness. That there is purpose in buying Christmas gifts for someone who is dying. I cannot believe that on this day everyone stops hating, that the lamb lies down with the lion, that the meek shall inherit the earth. Or that my father and Mother's father and mother and all their parents are standing by, just waiting. Nor can I believe in the words of John Donne. I cannot believe that in the end that Death does not win.

Christmas was a lonely time. My brother described it as one of the coldest days he had ever experienced. My journal entry totally reflected my current state of mind. Spiritually, I was all over the map, living in states of extreme belief, extreme doubt.

As Mother approached her last days on earth, Father Brady and others became obsessed with the act of anointing her, once again fearing that the devil was waiting to take her dying soul. I'd stand and watch from the doorway or from Mother's bedside chair, just about to lose my mind. At one point, I feared that if Father Brady or my first cousin Glady anointed Mother with holy oils much more, Mother was more likely to die from drowning long before the cancer succeeded. I began to question the shelf life of the oils—surely to God their effectiveness lasted longer than half a day. My mother was by far the most caring person I had known; she loved everyone in her path; she wouldn't have harmed a soul. I was certain that with the number of people dying on a daily basis there were easier pickings for the devil to find—not to mention that I didn't believe in the devil.

The absurdity of this situation came to light one evening when Mother's health had deteriorated, and the family had been called in.

Father Brady had been away delivering a retreat and was late arriving to the hospital. A nun who knew my family and volunteered at the hospital was making rounds, visiting the sick, and came to see Mother, who happened to be extremely low at that particular time. Spying the bottle of holy water on the neighouring bedside stand, the nun proceeded to say a prayer for the sick and dying, and as she prayed, she sprinkled holy water (yet again) upon my mother. As faith would have it, my uncle arrived at this very moment and proceeded to get quite irate upon witnessing her actions. The nun immediately replaced the holy water and excused herself. Father Brady continued to fester in a state of fury and disgust, which he clearly struggled to suppress. Unable to control his anger, he turned to me and spoke out against the nun; he was infuriated because this woman "did not know her place" and was acting the role of a priest. In his eyes, the nun had defied his position, and she clearly did not understand that her role was one of support.

Father Brady was speaking to the wrong lad.

In my eyes, it was yet another example of hierarchal and formalized rituals to which I could not relate. I admit that the nun in question was quick to get her hands on the bottle of holy water when there was no priest around and was equally quick to put it down when one did appear, but that was far from the real issue. First and foremost, the Sister was only trying to help. She had faith. She was a lovely, beautiful soul.

My uncle, however, continued to press the matter. I accept that he was only trying to do what he believed was right, what his training in the Catholic Church had taught him. He concluded our conversation by assuring me that women were never, ever, supposed to be priests.

I may have loved my uncle, but I had no time for that manner of thinking. I could not help but think of my days in Charity, Guyana, and the spiritual essence of the Sister performing mass to a congregation full of love. I asked myself which instance was truly more Christian, more humane.

Mother had been blessed with a beautiful friend and neighbour, Bernice Doucette. Towards the end of Mother's life, when she was at her lowest, Mother required little in terms of interpersonal relationships. For such a social being, this was a time when she asked for a reduction in visitors. Bernice was the exception. I would watch the pair from the doorway. It was pure, unconditional love. The communication between them was more non-verbal than verbal. Bernice would sit in the quiet by Mother's bedside, sometimes holding Mother's hand in silence, sometimes whispering a prayer or reading, bringing water to Mother's parched lips, just being with her and assuring Mother that she was not alone. Bernice was a presence that brought Mother a degree of peace when few else could. She allowed Mother her sorrow when Mother needed it… something that came easily between the two of them.

I was enthralled with the power and beauty of this friendship. As a child, I myself had always felt protected around Bernice, but I never understood the depth of her spirituality, not until many years later. Like my mother, she was a model of caring/compassion in action.

It was during one of those last visits, when Mother and Bernice were alone, that Mother suddenly roused from her slumber and pointed to the air as if towards an invisible presence and spoke my father's name—it was as if she had received a deathbed visit from her departed husband to help ease her transition to death. Though I wasn't present, it warmed me to hear this story afterwards. My mother died in a rather calming state within a few days.

Bernice left me with many a beautiful memory and lesson.

At the time of my mother's death, I wished all too well that my courage had not failed me, that I had been willing to share my past with her. The secrets that I wished I had shared were not of my father's past; rather, I wished I had had the courage to share every aspect of my spiritual experiences. I wanted to share how messages came to me, that authentic source of energy, for it was those experiences that allowed me to know that there is, indeed, much more to life. At the time of my mother's death, I wanted her to know that though I did not know what happens when we die, I believed in far more than the physical domain we were living in— that this is not the end—that there is far more than I could possibly conceive. I still agree that only good could come from sharing beautiful moments, by acknowledging my beliefs, by being completely honest with my mother. What could have been lost? What could have been gained?

I wanted to share, but I had always known that Mother wasn't open to supernatural or psychic discussions.

So I said nothing.

I really thought her attitude might have changed towards the end, but then she never even spoke again of the statue experience.

I just had to say something, but I didn't. I didn't take the risk. I remained quiet.

Imagine. Who wants to live their life like that?

The chance was lost.

It was one of my few regrets.

In the Gospel of John, there is an account of the time when Jesus was invited to come and see the body of his close friend, Lazarus. John simply states, "Jesus wept."

It is the shortest verse in the Bible.

And it shows us how God/Spirit responds to our suffering.

Jesus's tears were a sign of his love.

There were no words to get in the way.

And when Mother took what I knew to be her last breath, though I had no proof of what lay ahead, I knew I had lost a great friend. I had also lost my strongest emotional, spiritual contact. Initially, there was a spiritual void as well.

"World without end, amen."

It was the morning of Mother's wake. I had spent the early hours alone and was now heading out to the wake, which was being housed in the newly renovated vestry of her parish church in South Rustico. Along the way, I decided to stop by and see my goddaughter, Chantle, who was five at the time and a constant source of delight in my life.

Michelle, my first cousin and Chantle's mom, greeted me at the door.

"Good morning, Adrian. Mom said you'd likely be by to see Chantle this morning." I guess they knew me well enough. Michelle paused for a moment. "I wanted to speak to you before you saw your goddaughter. She's a little confused."

"In what way?"

"I'll let you see for yourself. I just wanted to... sort of prepare you."

I watched Michelle go to the top of the stairs, lean over the railing, and call down to her daughter, "Come upstairs, Chantle, your godfather is here to see you." Turning to me, Michelle said, "Ask her where she's going today."

Death can be difficult to come to terms with at any age. Michelle felt that it would be best if Chantle, as young as she was, was included in the grieving process and ceremonies.

As Mother's illness progressed and the days of communicating and responding to visitors were over, Chantle began to voice her frustration, questioning why her grand-aunt did not continue to visit, or why I did not take Chantle to the hospital to colour by Aunty Etta's bed like I had done previously on the occasional Saturday. For now, I watched as this whisper of a child bounced up the stairs, bounded into the kitchen, and jumped into my waiting arms.

"Don't you look beautiful, princess."

"Thank you."

"Why are you so dressed up?"

"I'm going to the *wake up.*"

I smiled and drew her little warm body in as close to me as humanly possible without smothering the poor child.

"The wake up," I repeated aloud.

Released, Chantle immediately ran back downstairs to whatever activity I had taken her from.

"The child may be in for a wee bit of disappointment," I said to Michelle.

Carrying on my way, driving the familiar rolling roads of my childhood, I replayed Chantle's words over and over in my mind. *The wake up.* I could not help but think of the Biblical passage Psalm 8:2: "Out of the mouth of babes and sucklings hast thou ordained strength because of thine enemies, that thou mightest still the enemy and the avenger." And the enemy I told myself was death, and now I knew that death, thou shalt not win.

I had no concept of what happened after death.

I found little comfort in speaking about the afterlife, because I had nothing to draw from: no concrete proof, no communications that confirmed life after death. While I refused to accept any doctrine on the grounds of blind faith simply because it has been told to me, I did welcome and remain open to hearing or reading other people's sharing of personal accounts of near-death experiences or unexplained communications. I was definitely intrigued.

In the preceding years, when I shared the experience of receiving a message while driving my car and everything that unfolded, of the few whom I shared with, many of them questioned me as to whether or not this might have, in fact, been my deceased father communicating with me. For it was only a matter of days since he had died when I received my message. I admit that it would have been nice to believe that this was my father communicating with me from beyond, but, in all honesty, that particular thought had never once crossed my mind. It was too big of a conceptual jump to go from an unexplainable communication to immortality. Regardless, it wasn't the answer that most people wanted to hear.

In all honesty, I could not say that my experience suggested or was proof of immortality or the existence of an afterlife; it was, however, evidence of the greater mysteries and miracles of everyday life. It was information coming through from another unexplained dimension. But I couldn't say where. Therefore, I did not speak about an afterlife because I did not know.

When the true content of any theory cannot be verified by scientific testing, then in the eyes of science, the theory can only be false. But this line of reasoning should not infer that the theory is untrue. It merely shows that the theory is capable of being shown to be false by the sole restrictions of repeated observation or experimentation. Verification is not possible. And, yes, I would choose medicine or assessments with predictable results every time... but predictable results are not always possible in all facets of life. Most scientists and naturalists can surely speak of what happens to our bodies when we die on this earth; that doesn't make them an authority as to what happens to our souls.

All I knew was that we are more than our bodies.

Part V

Coincidence is God's way of remaining anonymous.

Albert Einstein

Pay more attention to your dreams, for this is where truths are given.

Edgar Cayce

IN JULY OF 1998, the summer following Mother's death, one of my closest friends and I travelled to beautiful British Columbia. It was my first trip to the west coast; I had never travelled past Banff. Alan and his family had been a tremendous support during the period of Mother's illness and death, and he and I had become quite good friends. Alan was attending a conference in Vancouver, so we flew out together with the intent of spending a few days touring the city before I flew on, farther north, to visit my cousin and her family in Terrace.

On the flight out, I picked up a copy of *The Globe and Mail;* that edition had an article on "spiritual destinations." Ireland and Wales were among the locations. The Dingle Peninsula was recognized as one of the greatest spiritual locations in the world: my favourite place ever. Wales was also noted for its mysticism, and it was one of the places Cheryl dreamed of visiting. I was greatly impressed and took this as a sign that this journey would be spiritual as well. I wasn't disappointed.

Vancouver was amazing. Alan and I were enjoying the city and each other's company. We walked everywhere: Chinatown,

Gastown, Stanley Park, and Granville Island. One day, we even hiked Grouse Mountain. I was feeling much more grounded and in tune with myself. Getting away, travelling, had been good for me.

The Queen Charlotte Islands and the Pacific Ocean lie off the mouth of Prince Rupert. From the harbour, an uncrowded road twists and turns, moving deeper inwards for miles. The town of Terrace, in northern British Columbia, is both beautiful and remote. I spent a week there, surrounded by mountains, swimming in the cold freshwater lake, burning the driftwood that washed in along its shore, and living and resting among trees and my relatives. I walked along the top of a mountain that still knew ice and snow in the warmest of all seasons. I spent more than one lazy afternoon reading to the comforting and neighbouring sound of lapping water. I spent Mother's birthday, July 12, with a childhood neighbour of mine who had moved there, fishing salmon on the Skeena River. An eagle flew overhead and a black bear, the first I had ever seen, ambled out of the bushes not far behind us. Before noon, I hooked a salmon only to see it rush the rocky bank and roll away to freedom. Perhaps it was meant to be.

One evening, my cousin, Lynn, and I were sitting on the rocks below her house, drinking our coffee, watching her two boys playing along the water's edge. With the sun beginning to set, she asked, "Have you ever seen a psychic?"

"No," I answered, half chuckling. "The opportunity has never really presented itself. To be honest, I likely wasn't very open to the idea, anyway."

I was drawn to the supernatural and the unknown, but the realm of mediums and psychics was not of my world. I certainly hadn't ever met one.

"I have a friend who is a psychic who I have gone to see. I went after your mother's death. I think you would like her." Now Lynn laughed. "She's not weird or anything."

"I'd try anything right about now," I answered, and I meant it.

Lynn arranged an appointment for later in the week. I drove myself into Terrace that morning in their family station wagon that Lynn let me borrow. The town was small, quiet, and easy to get around. It was easier still to move about, as no one knew me. I was an internal mess, so anxious and nervous, but I carried on. Seeing a psychic was way out of my comfort zone. On some level it felt like I was betraying my mother and her church's beliefs. Though I couldn't name the process at the time, what I was doing was questioning my old belief systems. I was trying to turn off my critical, sceptical mind and force it to accept new ideas about life and death—challenging beliefs that I had long held on to.

The psychic worked from her home, which was just outside of the downtown centre. She greeted me warmly at her front door, and I followed her into her home. I took a seat opposite her at the table, and she immediately began. She spoke of shamans and Celtic ties and shared a brief history of her own. Then she took a new direction and spoke to me of guides.

"You have an old soul," she said, but to me her words held the nonsense of a foreign language. "It is a soul of great knowledge that the teachings of society have blocked from you. You are different and have felt so all of your life.

"You have a strong aura, blue in colour. It's stronger than average. Unfortunately, this makes you extremely sensitive to others' emotions. It can make crowds and unnatural settings unpleasant."

She proceeded to explain the implications of this blue aura, and I just smiled and listened like a child at a fair. She spoke of dreams and teachings. "Dreams are very important to you and have been even as a child. You will receive many teachings through them." I thought to myself that she could repeat these phrases to anyone.

Then, she told me that there was green along my throat and that I needed to work on verbalizing my beliefs.

"You are a teacher. Do not expect that everyone has the knowledge. Writing will definitely help, but it is not enough."

The woman then spoke of my stomach, saying I needed to allow my feelings to become stronger. "Feelings," she said, "are different than emotions. It is too easy for you to resort to your mind or intelligence and to analyze your feelings. There's a real knot there. I interpret this as unfinished business."

Then she was silent for a minute. In the silence, I sat wondering if my inner discomfort was that obvious and visible.

She questioned that while my heart and mind were open, why did my throat glow? She knew there was something I needed to say.

"Your greatest block or threat is your own fear. There's a tremendous fear of rejection, of not being accepted. This stops you from taking risks. You care too much about what society thinks."

The psychic continued to speak about related themes and came back to the subject of fears. She urged me to trust my intuition. "It has served well in the past. If you will trust your inner knowledge, it will be correct.

"You have too many unfulfilled ideas. It comes back from a failure to take risks. You have knowledge, but lessons are further learned in action. Learn to play again—remember what play really is. Act more spontaneous and creatively.

"You are a teacher, and that role is different than that of guidance. Again, do not expect that everyone has the knowledge—your purpose is to teach that there is no difference between the worlds of the physical and spirituality. Both can be readily attained. You must differentiate between spirituality and religion. You have this knowledge." I immediately recalled an experience I had as a teenager in church, when the priest prayed for writers who would tell of God's glory. I had told myself that morning that someday I would write a book celebrating his/her love and I would differentiate between spirituality and religion.

It was a lot to absorb. I was mentally overwhelmed. Then she took out her tarot cards. The cards supported all that she had said.

"You will be ridiculed and rejected by many, but of what value is their opinion? Your reputation and sincerity will help you. What do you have to lose?"

My reputation, standing in my community, family, friends…

Then she returned to the topic that had initially captured my attention.

"There is definitely some unfinished business. There's also a special woman in your life. Share your knowledge and unfinished business with her. She will understand."

Then she mentioned my mother, saying how she had passed on and was doing well. "She is busy doing other things. You need to bring closure, and this is what your mother wants.

"The recent spiritual blockage with your mother's death was a lesson—abilities do not go away but can be put aside. You will be prone to depressive states, but these should also serve as a lesson— it will be difficult to always see this, to know what these states are telling you. Pay closer attention to your body and emotional states—what are they telling you?"

At the completion of our session, my psychic paused, then smiled warmly. That's when she really got my attention.

"You could do this work if you were willing to learn."

"I'm flattered," I said, "but it was a world unknown to me; I would have had no idea of where to start."

"Remain open" was the only advice she left with me.

I struggled to believe that this was real. I would have welcomed something much more concrete. I was not convinced that the event was one hundred per cent real, nor would I have ever called her a fraud. What I could not deny was that I felt different, that she had touched something deep within me, that I was experiencing a new sense of peace. Her words and insights had helped me look at things from a new perspective. The experience gave me the fortitude to move forward and to make a change. I was not going to deny that it did.

That evening, after my session, I took a long walk along the shore that bordered Lynn's home, tracing the source of water that fed into the mouth of the bay, walking into the woods until I came upon a waterfall and could not go any farther. A tree had fallen across the river. I climbed its broken back and crept out until I came to rest somewhere near the middle of the rushing water. I sat there for ages, dangling my legs over the rushing water, sitting some eight to ten feet above its surface. It was at that moment that I felt my mother's spirit in the water's essence—water that flowed from an original source, being thrust into this world, taking the form of life from the powerful falls, in time eventually settling in the calm of the bay with parts leading off to various sources, watering, without judgement, all in its wake, touching many aspects of other lives, and in time returning to its original source.

I had no concept of where my mother was and had no right to know. She had moved on. But I was listening to the whispering voice within me.

It was time to bring about closure... to let go.

On the waters of the Skeena River in Terrace, BC, I had said goodbye to my mother, and in a hotel room that overlooked the Pacific waters of Prince Rupert harbour, I began the same process for my father. It was only with Mother's death that I found the freedom to address and resolve my own dysfunctions. With Mother's death, I buried both parents. Once returned to the tides of the Atlantic Ocean, I was determined to face my past.

Father had angled our house to allow the best view of the ocean. From the living room window, you could see Robinson's Island creeping out into Rustico Bay. I had been back home on the Island from my trip out west two days when I called Cheryl, asking her to meet me there. We sat on the shore bank that looked out on the Gulf of St. Lawrence, the hot July sun on our backs, our feet tucked into the warmth of the sand. Fishing boats were returning to harbour after the afternoon tours of deep-sea fishing. Flocks of seagulls hovered near the ships' sterns, swooping down in hope of catching some filleted fish remains that were being tossed overboard.

"My father was gay," I said, breaking the silence. In the nine years since he had passed, I had never once shared Father's sexuality with another soul. Suddenly, I didn't feel so alone.

Though the truth was that I was never alone.

I told Cheryl about my childhood home, the enmeshment and secrecy. It felt like a weight had been lifted from my aching shoulders and was sent out to sea, that the veil that had darkened my perception for the past nine years had finally been lifted. I was tired of fighting a ghost.

"My father was gay." I spoke the words again, only more softly. For the first time in my adult life, I felt completely honest. Yes, there was relief and honesty, but still a part of me felt I was betraying my family—so ingrained were my family beliefs. Thank God, I believed that the truth was healing. I guess that's what healing pain means. Cheryl let me talk before reacting.

"That son of a bitch. I'm so mad at him. How could he have lied to and betrayed his family? Your poor mother. She didn't deserve that."

"It all makes sense now, doesn't it?"

In the Gospel According to Thomas (70): "Jesus said, 'If you bring forth what is within you, what you bring forth will save you. If you do not bring forth what is within you, what you do not bring forth will destroy you.'" For the first time in my life, I felt like I was able to fully live out that revered passage.

But an even stronger association arose within me.

I was truly living out the "spiritual message" of my childhood; that voice was telling me that s/he did not want me to live my life in a lie, not ever. On the shore of Robinson's Island, in the company of my future wife, I told myself, "This is exactly what that voice wanted of me." It was the dawning of a new spiritual truth, that I would only know real love when I let myself truly be known.

After telling my story and feeling the taste of truth, I was ready for the next stage of my journey. I made the decision to go for professional counselling. Having given up my secrecy, I began to notice another reality; as I tasted truth, my intuition returned. I was about to enter a period of increased intuitive awareness in my day-to-day living. There was no way these two happenings—living the truth and intuition—were not related.

As I started back to work for a new school year, I received some subtle reminders of the importance of presence and simple acts of kindness. I had gone to the gym with a friend, and, afterwards, we were cooling down in the outdoor hot tub. A young girl joined us. She smiled warmly and sat there listening to my friend and me rambling on with each other.

Finally, she interrupted us. "Excuse me, but what do you work at?" she asked me.

"I'm a school counsellor."

"I'm so glad to hear that." I could tell she truly meant her words.

"Do I know you?" I asked.

"You wouldn't remember me. I was in grade six when you did your practice teaching."

My friend attempted a joke, implying how that teaching experience must have set her back, but she quickly responded in my defence.

"My best friend and I had found a male we could trust—for my friend, it was her first time."

There was a bit of a pause as we all absorbed the meaning of what she had said. I sat there listening to the white noise of the traffic down below.

The young girl wasn't finished. "We loved your honest affection."

"Thank you for sharing that."

The second incident came at a wedding dance I was attending. A former classmate of mine was walking towards me, smiling. I recognized her and smiled back. We were never especially close.

As she drew in close, she stopped and asked, "Do you mind if I hug you?"

"Of course not," I replied.

"Your kindness got me through grade nine—the worst period of my life. You were the only popular student who ever spoke to me and made me feel worthy."

Her words sent chills down my spine. In my eyes, I had done nothing, absolutely nothing.

These two seemingly unrelated incidents spoke of the beauty of simple acts of kindness, of the innocent power we all have to affect one another. These were simple gestures on the parts of these two females, but it took strength and courage for them to be so open, so vulnerable. My acts may have helped them in the distant past, but their words made a world of difference to me in the present when I needed them most, when I was struggling to find meaning. There is tremendous power in kindness, and, apparently, it doesn't have to be complex or elaborate to have lasting, meaningful effects. As my former student reminded me, they simply need to be honest and sincere. Our simple acts of kindness had touched us equally. What we do to others, we really do to ourselves. The joy of others can be your joy.

A month had passed. I was having a very difficult time at work. It was a combination of factors including the mounting workload and the number of complex cases. I was working at Charlottetown Rural High School filling a one-year leave in the student services department. So everything was new. It had been my worst week since the beginning of the school year.

That morning the student services administrative assistant knocked on my door.

"A present just arrived for you. It's on my desk."

What the hell could that be? It's November. Missed my birthday, too early for Christmas.

I stepped out of my office and followed her. There on her desk was a beautiful, small bouquet of flowers.

"They're for me?"

"That's what the card says."

"Thank you."

I grabbed the flowers and was returning to my room.

"Don't forget the card."

In the privacy of my office, I opened the card. The flowers were sent from a single parent whose son I had worked with at my previous school. The note simply read, "Thinking of you." Then below in brackets, in her handwriting, the parent had written, "I sensed that you were having a bad week. Just acting on my sixth sense."

That felt amazing.

I wasn't alone in my thinking. Other people trusted their intuition as well.

My one-year assignment was half over. It was the middle of February, so I had to make the decision of whether or not I would be returning to my former assignment. It was a great school, with great staff; however, inside of myself, it felt like I was moving backwards.

Monday, February 15, 1999
Richmond St.

Last night, I dreamt I was a pilot. I had an unknown co-pilot with me. The weather was bad. We were at ground level and I knew take-off was going to be difficult.

My co-pilot said, "I'm always here to take over when you need me."

I was pulling back on the controls, forcing the nose of the plane upwards. There was tremendous shaking as if the plane might implode. I was visibly shaking as well and sweating profusely. The co-pilot remained calm and composed.

We never crashed. We rose up, but soon needed to make an emergency landing. There was a high flat building in the horizon, so we landed on its roof. I was physically and mentally exhausted. Ironically, the building was an extra-large school. There was a gymnasium and several classrooms... from above, the classes looked like cells.

Rested, I prepared to leave again… the co-pilot still by my side.

I had been seeking some inner guidance and direction regarding my upcoming decision to leave the security of the school setting or not. A big flight wasn't easy for me. I had been struggling, not allowing anyone to help. That had to change. With my co-pilot by my side, I made the decision and passed in my notice. I knew enough to take a year off from work and to open myself to new possibilities—to take a risk. I was going to listen to my soul. For one year, I was not returning to my former school or to any school for that matter. I was taking a leave with no destination in sight. I was taking a risk. I trusted my inner voice… but not enough to speak openly of it.

Webster defines *coincidence* as "a remarkable concurrence of events or circumstances without apparent causal connection." These so-called coincidences continued and continued to transpire in my life. I began to view these events more as *synchronicity*, a term first explained by psychoanalyst Carl Jung as "events that appear significantly related but have no discernible causal connection."

Clinical neuropsychologist Dr. Mario Martinez defines synchronicity as "coincidental coherence that supports your actions by presenting conditions of timely significance." To him, these coincidences were vivid reminders of the interconnectedness of life. These experiences confirmed that we "are not some sort of Darwinian accident living in a world of meaningless existence."

The gifted medium Theresa Caputo beautifully refers to synchronicity as learning to read sign language. Life will offer confirmation if you are on the right path.

Some days, we are the teachers; some days, the student.

Everything in life was a gift. All of life was a miracle. There was meaning in everything.

With the decision finalized, I took off to Halifax with my brother and some friends for a weekend of music and partying. Inside, I was still very anxious about my recent decision. It was late by the time we crashed on Saturday night, but I couldn't fall asleep. My brother was snoring relentlessly. I slept for a brief spell but couldn't settle. I tossed and turned, watched some television, read a bit of a book on Buddhism philosophy—all to no avail. I kept getting the same thought. *Get up… go for a walk… go to Tim Horton's down the street.* But it was only five o'clock. Finally I gave in.

Tim's was quiet at this hour on a Sunday morning. There was one young lad sitting by himself. I asked if he minded if I joined him.

Thomas was nineteen, a high school dropout, single child, and recovering drug addict from a broken home. He generally didn't sleep much, he said. He shared that he was leaving in a week to attend a Buddhist retreat in Cape Breton. He had committed for a year.

We spoke for two hours. He needed to talk; I mainly listened. We shared our beliefs on death, religion, spirituality, and values. At his relatively young age, his life lessons had already taught him that he needed to start believing in himself.

"I'm so thankful that I had such a severe drug problem," he said.

"Really."

"It forced me to get help. It forced me to finally look at myself."

In 1999, I finally self-published *Spiritual Harbours: Honouring Healthy Dependencies*. It was supposed to be the good book—the book that would recognize the parenting my father had done and honour my relationship with him as well as his teachings, as opposed to the book I knew I would eventually write about the harm of his secrets and betrayal.

Tuesday, July 5, I held a book launch. It was a moving experience. There were so many people from my extended family, childhood community, work, and other agencies. I could hardly speak as a result of the emotion.

However, I was also moved by the synchronicity of the event— on the same night, twenty-two kilometres away, in St. Patrick's Church, there was a celebration for the eight priests who had come out of Fort Augustus, my father's rural childhood community. Had my father stayed in the seminary, he would have been celebrated that same night in his childhood church along with his bother; instead, on the very same night, Father was being celebrated as a parent through my book.

A friend from the education system read my book, and he suggested that we meet for a drink to discuss it.

"I enjoyed your book," he said. "I honestly did, but you're holding back something. I don't think you are being completely honest."

I said nothing.

"I don't mean to sound too critical, but your writing lacks a sense of rawness that I expected from you."

Holding back something... now that was a bit of an understatement.

Of course I was holding something back; he was absolutely correct in his observation. I was writing a book to honour my father while simultaneously trying to deal with the sense of betrayal and shame I had been hiding for over eight years.

At that moment, I became aware not just that my writing was inauthentic, but just how inauthentic I was myself. How could it conceivably have been an honest, open book? Whether you call it personal struggle or resistance, I had removed the antagonist, the villain.

My plans to take a year off from work didn't last long. Before the end of August, the Eastern School District board office approached me with an offer to develop an alternative school for severely behaviourally challenged elementary students. It was an excellent opportunity and a challenge that I felt I could not turn down. Simultaneously, I was offered a one-year, part-time pilot project as Educational Liaison Manager and Consultant with Child and Family Services (which is now referred to as Child Protection Services). At the time, I was the only frontline worker who did not have a social worker degree. My primary role was to case-manage problematic youth referrals from the school system and to develop and coordinate a Community Outreach Workers Program (youth workers). Through this work, I acquired an immense appreciation for social workers, and met some of the most spiritually minded people I would ever meet. I was touched by the degree of compassion that several of the staff embodied.

One day as I was leaving work at Child and Family Services, a crowd had gathered in the common room. A nine-month-old baby had been taken into care at the end of the day... an abusive father, an ineffective mother. There were no foster homes available. I watched as these workers' hearts were readily exposed. They asked me if I wanted to hold the child. Of course I did. The poor child was stiff—there was a failure to thrive. I had read too many studies that claimed infants who did not receive love would waste away and die. Inside of me, every cell of my heart was breaking for this child. I thought of all of the children my mother had welcomed into our home, and how she loved each one dearly. Everyone—the social workers and supervisors—stayed after work hours that evening until a suitable arrangement could be made. The humanity of these people was immeasurable. This was truly a spiritual harbour.

As far as immediate family, there was only Hayden and me left. With Mother's death, my brother and I were now midlife orphans. I wanted us to do something special, really special and meaningful. I eventually convinced him to travel with me to Ireland. Travelling always rejuvenates me. It is a chance to live life to the full, experience as many emotions as possible. The newness is stimulating; my mind and body awakens.

We made plans to rent a car, tour the countryside, and visit our paternal ancestral roots. Our father's ancestors hailed from counties Caven and Monaghan, so after picking up our car at the Dublin Airport, we headed due north. The first day, jet-lagged and exhausted, we drove as far as the Hill of Tara in County Meath. The Hill of Tara and the surrounding landscape were unbelievably beautiful. We both knew immediately that we had made the right decision to travel.

The next day we stopped for gas outside of the town of Monaghan. The attendant was really welcoming, so I struck up a conversation.

"How far is it to the city of Monaghan?"

"Have you forgotten?"

"I'm not from here," I said. "I'm from Canada."

"How long have you been away?"

"No, I'm from there. I was born there. I'm Canadian."

My brother had walked a short piece from the car and was smoking a cigarette. The lady pointed at him and said, "No, he's from Canada. You're Irish."

I laughed at her.

She said, "I'll prove it to you. Come with me."

I followed the lady inside of the crowded store, which also served as sort of a local tourist information centre. Another lady was behind the counter folding embroidered tea towels.

"Mary," my new friend called out, "who's this lad?"

"I can't tell you his name," she said, "but he's definitely a Smith from Monaghan."

It was indeed a strange sensation to be in a foreign land, and to be walking among strangers whom I looked more like than my neighbours and even most family back on the Island. My earlier feelings of connectedness with Ireland had been renewed and validated. In many ways, it felt like coming home. There is definitely something to be said for feeling spiritually connected to a land.

A friend had been into my workplace to see me. Through her work, Shelley was being offered the opportunity to start up a youth group. I strongly encouraged her to go ahead with this project. The only area that I emphasized was making sure her staff was well trained to deal with the emotional issues that were sure to arise. Ultimately, because of staffing concerns, my friend had to turn down a few high-risk students.

The following Thursday, Shelley left me a voicemail. The group had been out to an adventure-based learning site; it was a complete success, and I could tell from her voice that she, herself, was on a complete high.

Then tragedy struck—one of the boys she had turned down for admission into the group had died that night.

Shelley was devastated. She tried to reach me at the office, but I had left for the day. She genuinely needed someone to talk to.

That evening, totally oblivious to Shelley's day, I drove over to the north shore, parked in the National Park's parking lot, and went roller blading along the highway that bordered up against the rolling sand dunes. Upon my return, I noticed that for the first time in my life, I had locked my keys in my truck. My cell phone was also locked inside. It was dusk, and even though it was early summer, there was not a soul around.

I noticed a pay phone over by the changing rooms, so I skated over. I picked up the receiver to see if it was possible to make a collect call, as I had no change. Then I heard someone call my name.

It was Shelley. She had driven her mom out to North Rustico and had decided to go for a walk along the shore, trying to decompress from her day. Was she ever glad to see me. Was I ever glad to see her. She walked and I skated over to her car. We talked for a while, she shared the tragic events of her day, and then she drove me home.

There was never any question in my mind that we were meant to meet and talk that night.

I was in Halifax seeing my therapist. I had taken my cousin out for supper and was on the way back to Parrsboro, NS, where I had been staying for a few nights housesitting at a friend's place, when I decided to stop at Chapters. I was browsing around the store, but nothing was catching my attention. So I asked myself to find a book that would help me with my own writing, my own form of personal expression. I was drawn back to a section of fiction where I had been before. I decided to look over the titles again. Eventually, I was attracted to a specific book that I had previously missed. It was a thin paperback, so it could have been easily overlooked. Standing before the rows of bookshelves, I opened it and immediately my soul told me that I had found what I was looking for.

The book, *I Could Read the Sky*, was a photographic novel by Irish writer Timothy O'Grady, with pictures by British photographer Steve Pyke. It was a beautiful, lyrical story of Irish emigration written from the first-person point of view.

The book was darker than how I wrote, but I loved its passion and rawness.

Later I shared with Cheryl, "I write in English but think in Irish."

Just as there are Irish versions of dance and song, there was an Irish style of writing that I hadn't considered. The book took everyday, ordinary events and looked at them through a deeper, meaningful lens. I felt it was telling me to see life for all it truly is, and then write the same way. If I was going to write, I had to be more honest, more vulnerable. I needed to be darker when necessary to truly highlight the good. My writing had to be a true extension of who I was, not how I wanted to be perceived. I could not settle for less. Like the book, I also had to live in the present.

I needed to write like I needed to live. I needed to live like I needed to write.

I loved the counselling experience. I only went for three or four sessions, but the process was making a difference. It had been such a sense of relief to finally ask for help, but I was emotionally exhausted from the process.

Overwhelmed and frustrated, I had gone to bed in the middle of the afternoon, left a note on the table for Hayden asking not to be disturbed, and called Cheryl from the bedside phone, telling her I loved her. I knew something was happening that I couldn't explain. I had no reference point to draw upon. I told her I'd tell her everything later when I eventually figured it all out. Then I unplugged the house phone.

I had never ever felt as remotely low in any other point in my life. I could understand how some people give up. It scares me even to think about it. As for truly leaving home, my travels had done little in comparison with the intense self-reflection and counselling process.

Though I did not realize it at the time, I was enduring a pure mind-body experience. I can't explain how the process works, how the body mechanically responds, the mental reaction, or the intrinsic design of the emotional catharsis; I just know that it happened. I broke out in an intense fever in the dripping humidity of a late August day. I had fallen into a deep sleep that lasted until I woke from the chill of an afternoon sweat that poured through my pores as if my whole body was crying. Then a burning sensation travelled through my body. My mental disturbance had created a fever as real as any infectious disease might. As I lay awake in bed, the heat travelled through my body, slowly working its way down from my head and into my shoulders, flowing through my chest and stomach, my groin, down my legs to the soles of my feet—burning off my illness. Then the fever was gone. It felt as if I had liberated the stored energy out of my body. When shadows are touched by light, they disappear.

Part VI

We shall not cease from exploration
and the end of all our exploring
will be to arrive where we started
and know the place for the first time.

T. S. Eliot

HAVING TASTED TRUTH and with a successful, pleasurable counselling experience behind me, it was time to move on with my life. I was now consumed with making the most of day-to-day living. With the dawning of the millennium year, there were four distinct areas that were influencing my understanding of spirituality:

- My career
- Organized religion
- My redefined sense of family
- 9/11

Though they were major entities on their own, like much of life, their true essences were intertwined, and their teachings built upon one another.

I began working that fall as a counselling consultant within the student services department for the Eastern School District doing crisis intervention and counselling consulting for forty-three schools. In addition, I was doing academic and psych-educational assessments, coordinating and supervising various alternative education programs, and representing education on various interagency programs and committees. It was both challenging and stimulating work. In fact, it was the best job that I have ever had, and it came at a perfect time. It allowed me an opportunity to reach out to a wide range of students and families.

Throughout my career, I had worked extensively with alternative education students and had discovered some of the most rewarding moments of my career. All of these students had been marginalized to varying degrees. No wonder they couldn't find success in the traditional setting.

All I wanted was to make a difference in my students' individual lives. I wanted them to feel good about themselves, to see themselves as the beautiful children that they truly were. Given their life experiences, it wasn't always an easy feat. Damaged people damage people.

Then through my work, in a relatively short span of time, two friends re-entered my life. Little did I realize that my true quest for questioning religion was just beginning. Both men shared that, as adolescents, their parish priest had sexually abused them. Emotionally, they were both a mess, but, fortunately, both were actively working on healing.

This was during a time when the media was releasing continuous outrageous accounts of religion-based sexual abuse, primarily of young, vulnerable altar boys, and I came to know that locally and globally the Church actively tried to protect the identity and careers of the abusers as opposed to caring for the well-being of the abused innocent. It was too much. It puzzled me that a priest could preach from the pulpit against the horrors of same-sex marriage, but not a word was spoken when young children were being violated by one of their own.

Where was the voice of reason?

Where was that cry of outrage?

The Church, it appeared, was willing to ignore and hide the truth.

Now the Church was the "Holocaust denier" that Norman E. Rosenthal writes about. The Church wanted their followers "to put the horrors" behind and move on. Where was the teachable moment? Why didn't these parish priests speak out about the horror and cruelty that these innocent altar boys were experiencing? I wanted religion to explore and expose its dark moments, not to use people's faith to barricade the doors.

One of my most inspirational religious writers is the heavily tattooed Lutheran minister and current pastor at the House for All Sinners and Saints, Nadia Bolz-Weber. In her second book, *Accidental Saints: Finding God in all the Wrong People*, Bolz-Weber writes that we have made a great mistake "if we use religion as the place where we escape from difficult realities instead of the place where those difficult realities are given meaning... church was never meant to be a place for escapism. It can and should be a place where we dive into difficult truths."

That was what I was searching for: the truth, as difficult as it might be.

I completely stopped attending church.

Like most people in the Western Hemisphere who were teenagers or older, I can remember where I was and what I was doing on that day when, a thousand miles away, extremists flew two airplanes into what was then the World Trade Center in New York City. On that unforgettable morning, I was working as a counselling consultant and was en route to a school when my administrative assistant called my cell phone, asked if I had heard the news, and then proceeded to fill me in. I continued my drive to Morell High

School, where I was expected to check in on a few students. The computer teacher had a free period, and he was watching the televised coverage on a large wall screen. One of the students I was planning to see happened to be sitting alone at the back of the room, likely having been put out of a class by his teacher. I joined him, sat on top of a neighbouring desk, and we watched as the destruction continued to unfold.

At one point, as the towers were engulfed in flames, the student looked up at me and said, "It kinda puts my troubles into perspective, doesn't it?"

That week, I was teaching Introductory Psychology at the local university. The topic I was covering that class was memory. I asked the class what they were feeling. What makes a memory?

We could all recall the visions that were repeatedly displayed on televisions and reported in newspapers. Two thousand, nine hundred and ninety-six people dead and over six thousand others seriously injured. In the name of religion. The privileged life of North America was shattered. Yes, a great many people already lived in despair, but the greater walls that collectively embraced us came tumbling down. War had washed up against our shores. It was the day that the God concept re-entered my head.

In his book *The Second Plane*, British novelist Martin Amis collects fourteen pieces of writing that examine varying depictions of September 11, 2001, and its aftermath. In his second article, "The Voice of a Lonely Crowd," Amis writes, "If God existed, and if he cared for humankind, he would never have given us religion."

The destruction of the Twin Towers was my first introduction to the potential realness of war. And it was miles away in a bordering country. And the enemy lived thousands of miles even farther away, but I had stood at what would soon become known as Ground

Zero at least twice before. It felt as if the war had been brought home, that we were not that far removed. My dreams became full of hijackers and other attacks.

In my journal I wrote: *"The world has changed, once again. I can only hope future generations will not have to live in such terror."*

However, it would be years before the full impact of September 11, 2001, would materialize fully in Cheryl's and my world.

In the days that followed September 11, all sorts of conspiracy theories, racism, prejudices, and outright lies would erupt. Perhaps the most disgusting was from Jerry Falwell, Sr., an American evangelical Southern pastor and televangelist who openly denounced the moral decay of Americans:

"I really believe," Falwell said on September 13, 2001, on a Christian television program, "that the pagans, and the abortionists, and the feminists, and the gays and the lesbians" helped make the atrocities of September 11 happen, "because God will not be mocked."

The equally questionable Reverend Pat Robertson responded in agreement, merely saying, "Amen."

The next day, on the fourteenth, Falwell apologized for his ugly comments, but the damage was done.

It truly comes down to our beliefs. Unfortunately, some beliefs are absolutely mad. It doesn't matter if it's Muslim extremists, Western fundamentalists, or Christian Crusaders; they actually believe in what they say they believe. The trouble was truly fanatics and their corresponding beliefs.

All religions can be seen as opportunities to express our beliefs and experience divinity from unique perspectives. We are simply drawn to different faiths and leaders. In accordance to their own words, nearly every religion and ethical tradition preaches a respect for a universal power and some dictate of the Golden Rule: "treat others as one would like others to treat oneself." They all speak of compassion, empathy, unity, and understanding. We are told to perceive and love our neighbours as extensions of ourselves. This is how we teach our children to play fair; this is how we can live harmoniously with one another. The fundamental concepts are the same; only the presentation is different: different paths to the same destination, all leading upwards. Or as the spiritual author Steve Taylor so beautifully writes, "different views of the same landscape."

How could we have gotten it all so wrong?

In the eye of evolution, whether a person is a Christian, atheist, Muslim, or Jew should hold little importance. Whether you worship in a church, mosque, or synagogue is irrelevant. A pure religion would only teach and practice acts of equality and respect, and, if worthy, it would be open to criticism and inquiry—open to questioning. Evolving as a human being surpasses all forms of religious faith.

Thursday, October 18, 2001
New Dominion

The Teachers' Convention was late this year. For once I decided not to attend the dance. I have spent enough years socializing aimlessly at these events. Tonight I was content to come home and complete mending the wooden fence. Bobby (our horse) comes home tomorrow. Cheryl is so excited. I worked on the fence and then came in, showered, and wrote.

Recently, Cheryl confessed to me that having had cancer at the age of thirty and with the financial strain of being a single parent to three children, she often questioned whether

she would live long enough to ever own a horse again.
Cheryl's health is good. She has her horse. Life is good.

Life was good. I wrote that journal entry before going to bed in the comfort of our bedroom, my body exhausted from the physical labour. Buying a horse for Cheryl was one of the greatest gifts I had ever bought for anyone.

With all the turmoil existing in the world, it was so important to take the time to acknowledge simple moments of happiness. It is far too easy to take life for granted. Instead, Cheryl and I celebrated our happiness of living together at every turn: hosting dinners for family and friends; taking our old yellow lab, Moody Dog, on long walks; renovating the attic, so I had a bit of a haven from the noise to read and write; following the boys in their sports; or playing competitive board games with the children in the evenings while drinking milky tea and eating ginger cookies. Our home in an old green farmhouse on three acres of land had become my biggest support at a level I had not known since childhood.

Though, if I am honest, my intuition was not as strong while I was overly engaged in the busy practicalities of daily life. Family was where I was directing my attention, so naturally that was the area I was developing in. I ultimately became conscious that even intuition could be taken for granted. The words of the psychic were playing out: abilities do not go away but can be put aside. Like physical health and relationships, intuition requires attention and awareness. For its truest depth, trusting intuition has to become a way of life.

It was now winter. Snow had been falling for days. There was little traffic on the country roads. The Island had literally come to a standstill. Cabin fever began to set in; I needed out of the house.

I got my snowshoes off the wall in the porch and called out for Moody Dog. Outside, the horses, covered in fresh snow, looked like they were wearing coats of white as they hung close to the entrance of their walk-in. Moody and I stopped briefly to acknowledge them before we carried on our way.

The sky held a special cast as the afternoon sun was fading under the cover of falling snow. We headed for the backfields. The snow had collected and was deep. It made for great snowshoeing. We eventually came to a grove of evergreens. I walked into the centre as Moody Dog ran under branches and around some trees.

And then it was as if time stood still. It was a gestalt moment. I was completely surrounded by trees, their branches laden with snow. I experienced a complete sense of peace, as if all was right with the world, of everything being connected, one with nature, one with God/Spirit. I felt no division between the dog, the falling snow, the trees, and me. The feeling of love was overwhelming. Moody Dog stood beside me, a layer of snow piling upon his back, tail wagging in delight.

No one judging. No expectations. No one asking anything of me. My heart full of love and joy. Life was perfect. I was perfect just being me.

Then it hit me. I was being loved unconditionally. Moody Dog's love was the love my Creator had for me. S/he loved me for being me. That was enough. Moody Dog, and all of the Labs that followed, would forever be symbolic of unconditional love, pure love—my Creator's love.

In that instant, standing silently in the quiet of the snow-covered trees, I saw my life differently. I was where I needed to be. I knew that I would never forget this feeling, and that it would be possible to feel like this again and again and again.

Everything is one.

It was my initial awareness that there are two worlds: the physical world in which we humanly exist and the spiritual world where our divine nature abides. And to be the best version of ourselves we have to be able to live fully, to self-actualize, in both worlds. And to move about, transition, between the two, and be fully present in whatever world presents at each moment.

Teaching Introductory Psychology as a sessional lecturer at the University of Prince Edward Island was a wonderful outlet for me as it allowed me, one evening a week, the opportunity to be back in the classroom. I had always enjoyed relating to students in this manner.

During the fall semester of 2001, one of my students suffered the loss of her mom. I heard about the death at the end of the week and was surprised to see my student back in class the following Monday evening. This young woman, who was in her early twenties, was a science major, and my credit was an accepted elective for when she applied to medical school the following year. That particular evening, I was lecturing on the topic of moral development. I welcomed my student back to class and offered my condolences before I began. To my surprise, later that night and related to our class discussion, the student shared that she accepted death and did not believe in an afterlife—nor did her parents. I said nothing for a moment. Clearly some of her classmates were uncomfortable with the openness of the conversation.

Prior to this particular night, I had only shared my Guyana experience with my closest of friends or with those people whom I came across that I instinctively felt might benefit from hearing it. I had never spoken of the occasion openly in the public. That evening, I felt moved to travel outside of my comfort zone and to share my experience in Guyana. It was not my intent to challenge my student's beliefs on the afterlife nor to imply in any way that my experience was proof of it; rather, my student was clearly a scientist, and I desired to know what her thoughts would be on my experience. Overall, the class was quite engaged while I spoke; however, this particular student simply smiled and nodded.

At the end of the semester, this student graduated with one of the highest, if not the highest mark in my class. She eventually went on to medical school. As she was passing in her final exam, she stopped to shake my hand and proceeded to share how much she enjoyed the class. I said I was sure that her mom would be proud of her. My student smiled and nodded her head in agreement. Then as she began to walk away, she stopped and turned back to me. She said the highlight of my class was the story of my experience in Guyana. She admitted that she really needed to hear that story, for it had challenged her scientific thinking on many levels. And I felt rewarded for following my intuition and sharing. I thought to myself that maybe more people might benefit from learning of my experiences.

Part VII

If the only prayer you say in your life is
"thank you," that would suffice.

Meister Eckhart

I have yet many things to say unto you,
but ye cannot bear them now.

John 16:12

I REMEMBER FEELING HAPPY with how my life was going: living with Cheryl and the boys, having all these animals in my life, my new career, teaching at the university. The reality was that while I truly loved my work, I began to feel extremely run down. I attributed much of this to the newness of the job and the demands and pace of the work; however, I did notice that I had far less energy after days I spent working in my office as opposed to days I spent on the road. That didn't make any sense to me; I would have expected the complete opposite. There was something about that building.

My body kept telling me to slow down. However, I wasn't listening. Then when I let my guard down, I took sick. I believe the years of emotional strain from living with my secrets had also taken their toll physically as well as mentally. I may have been happy with the pace of my life, but my body wasn't.

One night I woke up from a deep, feverish sleep. I sat upright in my bed. Cheryl was sleeping soundly beside me, and Moody Dog was asleep at my feet. I had only been asleep for a few hours. The wind was blowing against the worn wooden shingles of the old farmhouse in which we lived. There was just enough natural moonlight to illuminate the bedroom. I had lit a fire in the kitchen before going to bed, so the room was warm as the flue passed through our bedroom, carrying warm air to the roof. I sat up in bed in a state of wonder. I had an instinctive knowing that my health situation was serious; it was much more than the "walking pneumonia" that I had been diagnosed with.

I was really listening to my body for once. I acknowledged aloud that I was truly sick—really sick. My illness was not passing. Spirit had directly intervened in my life. It was a wake-up call. I accepted the severity of my illness. I knew I had to start devoting real time to healing.

By mid-June, I was off work indefinitely. Fortunately, working in the school system, I had the summers off. By summer, I was at outpatients at least every second weekend. My body was hit so hard that I spent the next four months basically in bed, sleeping twelve to fourteen hours at a stretch and resting throughout the day: in my bed, on the living room couch, or, if the weather was pleasant, on a reclining deck chair outside in the heavenly shade of our apple trees. Moody Dog was always by my side. However, no matter how much I slept, I never felt rested.

The other major symptoms I experienced were headaches, sore throat, a burning sensation in my eyes, and difficulty concentrating. To compound the situation, I soon began to feel irritable and depressed. My illness was now affecting those around me, and I was feeling sorry for myself. I couldn't help but think of my father's symptoms: brief lapses in memory, a lingering headache, and changes in his mood. And I knew all too well how his situation ended.

There's a reason a book on spiritual truths devotes a focus on physical limitations. That's the thing with spiritual insights: sometimes the message or insight is acknowledging that what you are doing wrong. I was currently living with all three types of stress—physical, chemical, and emotional—at the same time. Your body can't sustain that; I don't care how spiritually aware you are. I share aspects of my physical state because the implications were blocking the depth of my spiritual awareness.

Animals are an excellent example of positive energy: if you give them sincere love, it comes back in multitudes. In the days that followed, no matter where I rested, Riley and Cheryl always made sure an animal was present. Before leaving for work, Cheryl would see that Moody Dog was resting at the foot of our bed and one, if not both, of our two baby kittens, Garth and Gary, were snuggled on my chest. She knew these were long days to be left all alone. I began to see animals in an even purer light. What excellent medicine and company these spiritual beings were.

When you are fighting an illness of any type, physical or mental or both, you have a responsibility to surround yourself with caring people. Human touch is essential for healing. Loving animals can have a powerful effect as well. Nothing helps a person heal better than love. Like a recent dream of mine revealed, it's all about energy. You need to surround yourself with positive energy while avoiding negative, dead energy. It's not always as easy as it sounds.

Mary Lou Morrison was one of those meaningful people who came into my life. She was my director at work. The year before I took sick, she gave a journal to each of her staff. She called it a "gratitude journal." The intent was that at the end of each day we were to write down three to five things that we were grateful for. I took it to mean various acts of kindness and appreciation for simple pleasures that are easily and often taken for granted. Cheryl referred to them as those special little moments that tend to get forgotten. That gratitude journal forced me to look for the positives in my day; it was a conscious choice, and I soon noticed that these positives were everywhere around me, waiting to be noticed, to be celebrated. The most divine moments were being captured in the most human ways and in the simplest, most innocent moments.

There were many days when the gratitude journal meant more, and times when it meant less. There were days while I lay for hours on end in bed, my head aching, my body drained of energy, where I felt that there was little to be grateful for; on those days, it was hard to find the positive. Yet on those darker days where I had to force myself to write, to find gratitude, that's when the process held the most meaning.

I was shocked that my father on his potential deathbed could ask, "Was it worth it?" Those words negatively impacted me for a long time. But as I wrote nightly in my journal, I became aware that that experience had compelled me to live a life I would both appreciate and feel grateful for. I would complete each day by putting in writing why my life was worth living, so I would never have to ask myself that question.

Regardless of how tough times seemed to be, I reminded myself that there was more to life than this illness. I had the memories of my spiritual experiences and the surrounding joys of the world to comfort me.

The gratitude journal would provide a lifetime of meaning.

One fall afternoon when my energy was good, with time on my hands, I took a drive into the city and visited a bookstore. I had been spending countless hours reading to help past the time. This day, I had nothing of particular reading interest in mind. While I was scanning the bookshelves, one book caught my attention. It was entitled *Going home: Jesus and Buddha as Brothers*.

The author, Thich Nhat Hanh, was a Vietnamese Buddhist monk and Zen master. At the time, he was unknown to me; however, I trusted my instincts and purchased the book. There was a section within the book on "Our True Home" in which the author writes about the spiritual concept of home, and how he finds home everywhere in nature: in our trees and in the sky. From where I sat reading, in my lawn chair, surrounded by apple trees, my yellow Lab resting nearby in the shade of one, and a stone walkway that my lover made that weaved through her garden, his spiritual concept was one I could dearly relate to.

Thich Nhat Hanh also shared that the Buddhists have a habit of referring to their spouse as "my home." That book and that section in particular seemed to speak to me at the time; it helped me more than any other piece of literature to prepare me for the journey that lay ahead.

Reading that book encouraged me to take the time and reflect on what the word "home" truly meant to me. I grabbed my journal, and this is what I wrote:

Home

The surrounding woods and white blossomed trees

The smells of the horse barn

Moody Dog, Jack Weasel, my cats, our horses and wild animals

Cheryl's flower gardens enclosed by apple trees

The water in the distance as we drive to and from home

The newly renovated loft that I can call my own

The children and the special individual relationships I have with each:

Carlye off to university with a passion for studying the human
mind,
Dennis wanting to join Peace Keeping and
Riley playing rugby
Playing cards and board games as a family
Home-cooked meals with family and friends
Saturday nights watching the Toronto Maple Leafs
My writing and reading interests
Fresh drinking water
My home is Cheryl.

On a spiritual level, I knew that a nurturing, loving environment would have the greatest impact on my healing. You couldn't buy that type of magic.

My entire energy system was connected. When any one of our systems—physical, emotional, mental, or spiritual—breaks down, our entire energy system is affected. My physical health was a reflection of my mental and spiritual state and vice versa. If I was going to be committed to healing emotionally and physically, it was illogical to try to treat the domains separately. I was convinced that getting healthy would be a holistic venture. To restore my health, I knew that I would need to involve body, mind, and spirit. If I was to heal, I could not ignore my spirituality. If I healed my spirit, my body just might follow.

Still, I was definitely not at a stage in my own development where I was willing to even consider that my illness might ever be perceived as a lesson in life—

Challenging me to connect with my unresolved issues;

Challenging me to look at where I was in my life and make changes;

Challenging me to determine what was truly important.

I wasn't there yet... not even close.

Sometimes we can't see the forest for the trees.

During my illness, I instinctively knew that I felt healthier when I was by the sea. The ocean always had a calming effect on me, and I needed this more than ever. And the salty air felt especially good for my lungs.

I went to see a naturopath, and she was wonderful—kind, compassionate, and very pregnant. I was so fortunate to be her last patient before she went on maternity leave. She put me on a strict diet and some supplements to help strengthen my immune system. She also encouraged the sea.

"Continue to exercise by the water whenever possible."

The second change that was really making a difference in many aspects of my life was that I started to meditate again. It was really helping with my sleep and quieting my mind. The renovated loft was perfect; I would sit in my window bay, on the wooden floor with a mat. Light a candle and just breathe. Most importantly, one or both dogs would always join me. It would revitalize me.

I meditated regularly in those days. I knew few other people who embraced my pastimes: reading, writing, meditating, and walking the dogs. My desire for individuality reminded me of my father.

When I was growing up, my father went walking every day, generally in the evenings after work, in an era when no one walked for the sake of walking. This was his ritual. He stood out, but it brought him a sense of mindfulness and peace, so he endured. It was a wonderful spiritual truth that he passed on to me.

While I was off sick, the deputy minister of education at that time declared my work building to be unhealthy—mould and asbestos had been discovered. During this same time, one of the administrative assistants who worked in our office building died of cancer. My own father had an office in this particular building when he died of a brain tumour in 1989. Mentally, it was a lot to absorb. Within the year, the district office was moved to a new location, and the old building was sold and eventually demolished.

In the fall of 2002, I saw a specialist who worked out of the QEII in Halifax.

"I don't think you have any idea how sick you are," she informed me.

The first thing she did was take me off of all medication that had been previously prescribed to me and instead I was to exercise daily, sleep when my body required it, and avoid any unnecessary stress. The objective was to naturally rebuild my immune system. It was the first time a medical professional was telling me to take responsibility for my health. She wanted me to put my health first and listen to my body. It was some of the best advice I had ever been given.

I confess that a large part of me was really angry, and, in her office, my words showed my frustration.

"I exercise. All the time. It's part of my lifestyle, and I still get sick!" I voiced my anger.

"Imagine how sick you would be if you hadn't been exercising."

That was yet another lesson that I needed to hear of the value of preventive measures, of not taking any aspect of health or life for granted. I may very well have been alive or at least less seriously ill because of the fact that I did exercise regularly and had maintained a physically healthy lifestyle.

It was the same with meditation.

At various points in my life, I meditated when I felt I needed it most—when I came home from Guyana and was experiencing situational depression; when I was first home on sick leave with my undiagnosed illness—and at these times in my life, my intuition told me that I needed to meditate and the practice served a meaningful purpose; however, in my faulty reasoning, I didn't think I needed to continue after I began to heal. In my eyes, meditation was painstaking and time-consuming; I was impatient, wanting to get on with my life. I had to fight with myself to remain still.

I lacked the self-discipline to practice consistently. I was still too immature to fully recognize the long-term preventive value in incorporating these practices into my lifestyle, of making a ritual out of these practices.

The specialist had two more points: "You also need to consider a different career, and try to take in some saltwater air." It was the second time that a medical professional had recognized the healing influence of nature, particularly the ocean.

Things happen for a reason.

Concerned about changing careers, I made the decision to apply to universities and study towards my PhD in counselling psychology. My therapist in Halifax was instrumental in this decision. I had made sound emotional progress with my counselling sessions and kept detailed notes. I still wrote in my two journals, and my intent was to use these writings and my research as the basis of a thesis. My therapist was certain that there was a dire need for counsellors, especially males, to work in this field. She was certain that I could have a private practice if I so desired in the future. At this stage in my life, I would also have welcomed a career in senior management, where I was away from the frontline demands of the crisis work.

I completed a draft of a manuscript dealing with the topic of homophobia as it related to learning about my father's past and promoting the concept of therapeutic journalling. I applied to the University of Toronto, where my father had attended. I had grown up mesmerized by a University of Toronto diploma that my father had framed and hung on the wall. The faculty was interested in my thesis topic, and I was fortunate enough to be accepted into their program.

I had finally slowed down. For the first time, I was truly witnessing the beauty and wonders of life in my own backyard, the sacredness in the ordinary. Everything was miraculous. It had been such a long time since I had felt so grounded. It was like living in two worlds that I was trying to blend together. I had a newfound joy for simple pleasures and being in the company of my family, while simultaneously my intuition and dreams continued to speak of otherworldliness; however, both domains spoke to me of spirituality. Yes, we were physical beings living in a material world, but we were also spiritual beings living in a spiritual world. The greatest beauty in life was when these two worlds merged.

If my health scare had taught me one thing, it was that I could not control everything. I made the decision then and there not to try to force anything. If it was meant to be, it would be. I would simply remain open to the signs.

I had stuck to my decision of not trying to force my career plans. Then in the early spring of 2003, I received a letter from the University of Toronto. My acceptance to a doctoral program had been deferred for one year. It was the year of the double cohort, when Grade 13 in Ontario was abolished—a time of financial gain for the university, and the undergraduate program needed to be expanded. The universe was telling me something. This was my sign that I had been waiting for.

The decision was made, but it was a hard one; I would not be returning to university. I was giving up on a dream for now, but I had to make a choice.

My health had not progressed as well as I had hoped.

I believed I needed Cheryl and the children's support more than I needed another degree.

I believed they needed me as well.

We all have choices.

Although I had accepted my decision, I still knew that I needed a career change. So I threw that out to the universe, and I waited to see what would stick.

The day the final decision had been made, I called Riley and asked if he wanted to go fishing in the rain. He said he would love to. Cheryl had made other plans, but she cancelled them to come with us. That outing, I caught one small fish, and my company didn't catch any. Just before we left, Riley fell into water that was higher than his rubber boots. We laughed so hard that evening, enjoying each other's company. *How could I possibly leave this*, I asked myself: *family, fun, and love.*

Hurricane Juan came and went, but not before blowing down all of our apple trees and about thirty spruce trees along our treeline. The noise woke me at three o'clock in the morning. I immediately went out to check on the horses. Cheryl followed closely behind and helped me shut the barn doors. The horses, standing strong, were wondering what the fuss was about.

Cheryl was devastated. She adored her little orchard. It had been one of the primary selling points that drew her to the property. She had created the most serene little sitting space among its over-reaching branches.

The following Saturday, a gang of able friends showed up to help us with the cleanup. The support was tremendous. There was an overwhelming sense of caring fellowship among these people. We worked from eight-thirty that morning until four-thirty in the afternoon. We could never ever have done the work by ourselves. To show our appreciation, Cheryl cooked up two lovely meals that day.

The beauty of community… spirituality in action.

In *The MindBody Code*, Dr. Mario Martinez writes of three societal archetypal wounds: abandonment, shame, and betrayal. He believes that he has discovered a healing field for each of the three wounds. "*Commitment* heals abandonment, *honor* heals shame, and *loyalty* heals betrayal." To be loyal was to be faithful to love or promise. For someone with commitment issues who had endured betrayal, without any knowledge of Martinez's theory, I was embodying his beliefs. Through the act of marriage, I was proving to Cheryl and to myself that I could be loyal to both our love and to my promise of marriage. Yes, life felt totally different afterwards.

People would ask me, "Is it any different being married?"

I could only speak for myself: it was a world of difference, almost difficult to explain. My life felt enriched, more meaningful. I had given my word to a wife and family. I had committed. The change was sudden. I was surprised by how different being married made me feel; I was even more surprised by how okay I was with this new feeling.

What a crime it is when people refuse to grow, when we do not do everything in our power to be everything for our partners, our children, our friends, and ourselves. I could have easily continued to live a very lonely existence, and I wasn't even aware of how lonely I was.

The theologian St. Gregory of Nyssa would say that refusing to grow was a sin. I would have to agree with him.

A month later, Cheryl and I honeymooned in Wales. While visiting one of the many beautiful hamlets or villages, we happened upon a glorious, historical church; it could very well have been a parish of the Church of England. The graveyard had a mystical feel about it, accentuated with ancient trees, cobbled paths, and weatherworn granite headstones. The grounds of the church were immaculate, and the cemetery enclosed by a stone wall fence. While walking along the rows of headstones, reading the various names and inscriptions, by chance I noticed a small, equally aged plot, a white fenced-in section just outside of the cemetery perimeter; here lay a collection of unmarked graves.

As I was standing there looking over the cemetery wall, the back gate to the graveyard opened, and a man carrying a shovel over his right shoulder passed through. I assumed he was the groundskeeper.

"Excuse me," I called out.

"Yes. Can I help you?"

"I'm just wondering why that plot is over there bordering on the cemetery?"

The groundskeeper paused for a moment and explained, "That particular section is on unhallowed grounds. It was an area reserved in earlier times for unbaptized babies and people who committed suicide."

"Really."

The man nodded and continued on his way.

Unhallowed grounds.

I was lost for words for those poor souls. Burial inside the churchyard must have been reserved for "Christians Only." The stone wall symbolized the boundaries of entry into heaven.

In my heart, I still believed that on many levels there was much to be gained from writing about my relationship with my father. My journal writing had been a significant part of my healing process. The possibility of using it for future studies still existed. The writing was a sincere attempt to put the past behind me, to move forward while taking the good with me. I truly hoped that my writing could make a difference—be one of those things C. S. Lewis writes about that when you actually learn how someone else has suffered and yet survived, it can help as you begin to crawl up from your pain and suffering. I wanted to provide a history of fortitude.

At long last, I persisted and decided to write a memoir, *Sins of Omission*. As my health started to improve, I devoted much of my free time to writing (I still didn't have the extra energy for much else). I sent off letters to various publishers, primarily within Atlantic Canada. A small company in Saint John, New Brunswick, showed some initial interest, and suggested an e-book.

It definitely wasn't what I wanted to hear. But that voice inside me kept telling me that an e-book was enough. And the message was a strong, persistent one. Eventually, I listened to my instinct and agreed to their terms. I had written the book for therapy as much as telling the story. The voice kept telling me that this was enough for now—it would be a good middle ground.

When we put sincere intentions out to the universe, the spiritual truth is that we often receive the experience that we need; however, initially, it may not be what we thought it ought to look like.

Life really began to take some interesting twists.

When I had applied to the PhD program at U. of T., one of the primary career fields they prepare you for is a position in senior management at school boards and other mental-health-related agencies. In the spring of 2005, the provincial government offered an incentive retirement package to eligible teachers. My director accepted. I applied for her position and won the competition. These two unrelated events—U. of T. delaying my program acceptance and my director accepting the retirement package—coincided to change my future. It was pure synchronicity at work.

Two years prior, I had promised myself that I would not try to control things; I would let it be. I had willingly thrown my future career out to the universe, trusted, and had waited. The larger purpose did not reveal itself until now. In the end, I had earned the job that I had hoped further studies might have provided. Though I had no idea at the time, that rejection letter had stopped me from going down the wrong road. Accepting this job was so far removed from relocating to Toronto to study. It made me so appreciative and aware of how much I loved home and the Island. I felt blessed to be in this position.

And I was still changing careers.

A few weeks after accepting the new position, Cheryl came home from work, walked in the house and, out-of-the-blue, asked, "If we could live anywhere, where would you choose?"

I responded instantly, "St. Catherines."

"Perfect. Get in the car. Some land just came on the market. I want to put the first offer in."

Though the land and surrounding area were breathtaking, there were two spiritual reasons why the property spoke to me.

One, at various moments in my adult life, in times of personal change, the image of a white horse running in an open field has visited me in my dreams and meditations, and the first being to meet us on the property was a beautiful white horse. When we walked down to the stream, the horse came sauntering down the neighbouring field to a small, worn, wooden bridge, situated over the running water that separated our neighbouring properties. The horse just stood there, staring at us, a beautiful white horse without any blinders.

In *The Four Desires*, Rod Stryker explains the Hindu word *shvetashvatara*: "*Shveta* is the Sanskrit word for 'white,' *ashva* means 'horse,' and *tara* means 'supreme, excellent, the highest or most choice.'" Thus the term means "the white horse that leads you to excellence or to the most supreme place." I just felt that this horse was telling me to trust my intuition.

Two, within the span of two years in the early nineties, I had two strong dreams where I was travelling with friends and looking for land. In both dreams, I was standing at the end of a quiet road looking down a long pasture. The land seemed to go on forever. In both dreams, the pastureland was located in a valley, and, at the far end, there was water. It was so peaceful and heavenly in both dreams. The only difference between the dreams was that in the first one horses roamed freely on the property, and in the second, a warm, friendly man had shown me the neighbouring property that he was selling. Dream one ended with my friend saying, "I don't think you'll ever be complete, unless you live in the country"; dream two ended with a reference to land being a "fountain of youth."

Standing on the far end of the St. Catherines Road, looking at this property—the sloping valley, the neighbour's horse hanging about at the fence, the water running along the property's lower edge—it felt like those dreams were coming through. The warm, elderly man who owned the property lived next door. This was 7.5 acres of untouched pastureland, in a valley surrounded by rolling hills, overlooking an estuary that flowed into a river. Like in my dreams, I fell in love immediately with the land.

In just over a year, the three goals that I had documented in my year's end journal had been fulfilled: change careers, build a new

home, and write my book. I had become director of student services on June 4, began building our house on October 27, and was
in the final stages of having my e-book published. Life felt good.

By now, we had no fewer than three yellow Labs and one cat to
keep us company. It was time for Cheryl and me to create a home of
our own. I was thrilled when our house number sign arrived: 1111.

In the coming days, I spent hours watching the changing perspectives of the surrounding countryside—the early stages of spring—
the views from different angles. I would leave our house thinking
of a work task ahead and the morning view of the river at the top
of our hill would stop me in my tracks. The oyster boats were out
early in the mornings. One day there were five boats in a row, the
men working in union, the sun rising behind them. The scene was
the epiphany of peacefulness and serenity.

Back then, the Dunedin Bridge was one of the last remaining
wooden bridges on PEI, its ancient wooden structure spanning
the Clyde River. I loved that old bridge. I would come home from
work and literally wait for that bridge to come into sight—it felt
like I was leaving one world behind and entering another once I
crossed that timber divide.

It is a great feeling when you come to a different place in life
and love where you are, when you don't require hanging onto your
past and missing it. It was time to expand this way of thinking to
other aspects of my life. Such as, who was I becoming?

I admitted to myself that I felt the world was once again in its
proper order.

Then, in the summer of 2006, my world crashed even further.

It was the beginning of a time that would alter my vision of my
father forever.

It was like starting all over again.

Part VIII

Life is a process of becoming, a combination of states we have to go through. Where people fail is that they wish to elect a state and remain in it. This is a kind of death.

Anaïs Nin

Self-inquiry is the most direct approach to truth.

Mooji

ON JULY 6, 2006, my mother's two sisters, Alice and Grace, arranged a visit with Hayden, myself, and our wives. I had just signed a contract to publish my book *Sins of Omission* as an e-book. At a recent gathering of my mother's family, my Aunt Grace told me she had shared the nature of my book. She told me that in a state of rage, an extended family member had disclosed an account of being a teenager and being sexually abused by my father while he stayed at my parents' home. Then out of nowhere another relative had spoken up. He shared that he had had a similar experience with my father, but had impeded the attempt. Now, gathered in my living room, my aunts were questioning if I would proceed with my book. I had no idea what to do with this revelation. It made me ill. I wanted it to not be true.

Then one weekend in the ensuing fall, a school counsellor came to visit me at my home. He wanted to talk privately and in person. He couldn't share details because of confidentially, but one of Father's former students, now an adult and parent to one of our current students, had also disclosed an alleged abuse allegation against my father during a case conference in front of two colleagues of mine.

The feelings associated with releasing my book and what I felt after hearing those allegations were polar opposites. Eventually, I conceded to my anger and slid into a depression that lasted for months. Learning of my father's sexuality had been a mere warm-up to this news. All of the past was mild in comparison to the anger that was presently exploding within me. I believe that our brains are indeed biased towards patterns, for once again I initially wanted to protect the families that worshipped him and to shelter my parents' extended families. Somewhere inside, a significant degree of me also wanted to protect my father's name and my own. The same old story, the same foolish beliefs, the same old self-defeating patterns.

The anger I carried was exhausting. For weeks, I came home directly from work and went straight to bed. All of my old doubts and fears returned with a vengeance. All of those associated emotions that I thought I had dealt with came crashing down again… now with a new, heightened, and intense fervour.

There was nothing spiritual about my behaviour.

There was nothing meaningful about my thinking.

At the time, I couldn't see that I was not a victim to these patterns; I was an accomplice. I was promoting secrecy, protection, and fears. Fortunately, I became convinced that these patterns were going to continue to manifest in my life if I did not take the time to learn what the universe was trying to teach me.

In Anaïs Nin's quote at the beginning of this section, the author speaks of how we can get stuck at certain points in life and wish to remain there forever, convincing ourselves that this place is safe or that change is simply too hard or emotionally difficult. Nin refers to this behaviour as a kind of death. There truly are so many ways to die.

Unfortunately, it was a kind of spiritual death where I lingered when I learned of the allegations against my father and consequently had to face the fact that my relatives wanted me to abandon my e-book publication—something I had strived so long to accomplish. Part of me wanted to run, to simply abandon my plans and just hide. I even tried to convince myself that escaping would have been an easy road to take.

My initial response was to put my head down and dive into my new career. It was too easy to become consumed—to become addicted to the adrenaline that was making me sick. I was a crisis junkie. The pace was anything but spiritual. My work was fulfilling that unhealthy need: a vicious, vicious cycle that I wasn't even conscious of.

Once again, by burying myself in another distraction, I could repress my negative emotions, but I was closing myself off from good traits as well. You can't simply select which emotions to suppress; my creativeness and my intuition also went into hiding. Living in a constant state of stress does that.

It didn't have to feel like starting over. But I allowed that to happen.

Neale Donald Walsch believes in the "Law of Opposites." In *What God Said*, he writes, "The moment you declare anything, everything unlike it will come into the space," but these "distorted forms" of what we originally conceived are not obstacles, but rather opportunities to empower people to move forward. He writes, "There needs to be a *contrasting* element for *any* element to be experienced." It is an opportunity to recheck your beliefs, a chance to personally verify are you moving in the right direction; in other words, your destination may be correct but you can now question, is this the right way of getting there?

Fortunately, I made the decision to proceed with the e-book. Cheryl was so supportive. I believed that if I stopped, I was once again denouncing homosexuality. Nothing would have changed. *Sins of Omission* detailed a story of family dysfunction and the harms of deception, but it was as much a personal history of growth and tolerance and learning to accept individual sexuality. It reflected how my father's concealment of his sexuality had, in fact, become a lesson for me in acceptance and humanity.

But in light of these recent allegations, an e-book was enough.

Dennis was not a child as he prepared to leave for Afghanistan; at the age of twenty-three, he was a young man who was trained to kill. Still, as late in life as it may seem in comparison to others, this was one moment that would identify me as a parent.

Dennis left for his tour in January of 2007, so Christmas of 2006 was especially emotional for our family. I'll not deny that I gave him a small Bible and a medal of St. Christopher like my mother had given me when I travelled to Europe; however, the gift that I was especially pleased to give was a family ring that I had a local jeweller by the name of Jeanette Walker create. Jeanette had designed Cheryl and my wedding rings, so I asked her to design a family ring based on them. The rings were important to me, as all of the children were living away, but it was especially important this year, as Dennis would soon be leaving on his tour to Afghanistan. No matter where he was in the world, no matter the circumstances he was enduring, I wanted Dennis to have a constant and physical reminder of his family and a symbol of my love for him.

The night before Dennis's departure, we gathered as family in Dennis's modest dwelling, one of many in a row of unassuming military town houses. His grandmother, far too old to be faced with this reality, tried to say a prayer at supper but was lost for words. We were all emotional trainwrecks. And I, far too overcome with the magnitude of my son's stirring emotions, had to leave the house for a spell and get some fresh air.

Earlier in the day, I had noticed a church just up from the main entrance to the base, so I set out alone in the frigid night air with the intent of seeking some degree of emotional sanctuary. I did not leave seeking peace or harmony, for I believed that on a night such as this those feelings could not exist for me. I had hoped the church might bring some degree of consolation.

It was dark when I arrived. The parking lot was vacant. Much to my disappointment the church door was locked. The symbolism only served to amplify my prevailing sense of loss. I was clearly reaching for my childhood comfort, reverting to what I knew best. I had come in search of my childhood God, and, finding the door locked, I was as disenchanted as ever. My beautiful, empathic son was about to go off to war—to shoot and kill strangers who would be trying to shoot and kill him.

Where was God/Spirit?

As I began to retrace my path, I noticed a large maple tree standing alone at the edge of the church property. The moon's full glory radiated down through the spaces between its leaves. It brought forth memories of the trees on my university campus that had brought comfort to me when I was Dennis's present age. How our times were so different. I stood there for ages, alone, time standing still, looking up at the moon within the protective covering of this tree, and I prayed.

And I did find peace—for the moment.

This was Dennis's life journey, not mine. I knew he was going to survive.

People have asked me what was the most emotional experience of my life. For the most part, I believe that they are expecting to hear of one of my parents' deaths. Some are actually surprised by the answer: no single event paralleled the actual day that Dennis departed for Afghanistan; it was pure hell.

The deploying soldiers and their families and loved ones had gathered in a massive hall. The abundance of emotions was overwhelming—those emotions being readily displayed but even more so those emotions that were being so poorly suppressed. Mothers crying, babies crying, loved ones holding back tears, confused children running aimlessly about, and so much unspoken anguish. Not an ounce of peace and contentment abided within that massive hall; how could it? I was incapable of resurrecting the tranquillity that I had found the night before. I could not possibly comprehend what our son was about to face. How could I? I had to accept that I had absolutely no control over the situation. Dennis was one of many trained killers leaving on a mission, and all I could say was "Be careful" and "I love you" and then hold his mother in my arms when she came apart. This was her baby.

As he boarded the bus that would transport him to his plane, Dennis looked more like a schoolboy venturing off to a new year at school, with his backpack hanging from his shoulders, but his world and ours were to be literally turned upside down.

Those months were heart wrenching. One day I was in my office at work, and Darlene, one of my administrative assistants, came rushing to my door. "You have a phone call. I think it's Dennis. I'll put him right through."

My phone rang.

"Dennis?"

"Hi, Dad."

"Where are you?"

He chuckled. "In a battlefield in Afghanistan. Some sergeant is out here with a massive cell phone and said I could use it. Not sure how long the reception will last."

We had to speak loudly as the connection was bad. I could hear artillery firing in the background.

"Did you speak with your mom?"

"No." He paused. "I didn't want to take the chance of being on the phone and something going wrong."

"That was good of you," I replied. He was as sensitive and compassionate as ever.

"How is everyone back home?"

"Great. Everyone is fine. How are you doing?"

"I'm doing okay. It's damn hot in this desert."

We spoke for a few minutes. I could hear the fear and concern and homesickness in his voice a world away.

"It's so good to hear your voice," I said, and then there was the loudest noise and the phone went dead.

I came out into our office hallway. "We were disconnected."

No one knew what to say.

We hung close by and waited. I was left to wonder if I had lost more than a phone connection. After twenty minutes, the call came through. It was Dennis.

"I can't talk," he said. "That shell felt a little too close. I knew what you must have been thinking. Give my love to Mom."

On Sunday, April 8, 2007, Easter weekend, six Canadian infantry soldiers were killed in a roadside bombing and a number of others were injured. It was the worst single-day toll in combat for the Canadian Forces since the Korean War. We had been told at the military base in Gagetown that families would be notified before media reported the losses. That fact brought little comfort. Again, we waited.

The next day, the army released the names. Dennis had been on tour at that time but in a different location. He was able to call; he was utterly devastated—all three of his bunkmates were among the casualties. He had returned that day from the field to an empty dorm. He was overtired and emotionally drained; still, I could not put into words how great it was to hear his voice.

Dennis was especially close to one of the boys, David Greenslade. Dennis wanted so much to grieve properly for his friend, but he was ordered back into the field, as death is a way of life in a bloody war.

Later that same day, the ninetieth anniversary of the Canadian National Vimy Memorial in France—a war memorial dedicated to the memory of the sixty thousand Canadian soldiers dead and missing, presumed dead during the First World War—was televised. The massive crowd was silent, as were Cheryl and I in our living room, miles away, weeping while listening to a fifteen-year-old fiddle player, Sierra Noble from Manitoba, play "Metis Prayer/ Warrior's Lament" live from the top of this majestic monument. Only birds were singing in the background.

The timing was incredible.

On that Easter weekend of 2007, it was difficult to find God/Spirit.

My days in Charity, South America, were a distant pass, and, at that time, I had returned home full of optimism with beliefs not unlike that of the mystic sage Ramakrishna, who opined that the common goal of humanity was that of spiritual evolution: be you Christian, Muslim, or Hindu, Ramakrishna believed that "all religions are glorious." Now, ten years later, I was forced to openly question the validity of all religions and not solely the one that I had been raised in.

Tuesday night, I went to bed exhausted. I was still experiencing a sense of survivor's guilt. Cheryl and I did not know how to react. We were so grateful that Dennis was safe, but other people's sons were dead; this was so difficult to acknowledge. Here I was, safe, loving my home, my family, my animals, my work, while Dennis was suffering, not to mention the families of the lost soldiers. I told myself that there could be nothing sacred or holy within any war. That was the one night I felt too guilty to write out my gratitudes.

I woke at three-thirty, feeling none the more rested. I ventured downstairs and stepped outside on the deck. The trees were clear and visible in the moonlight. I reminded myself that no good would come from feeling guilty and angry, that I would only attract bad energy. I could not control the situation in Afghanistan, no matter how many hours and days or years I festered, but I could make a sincere effort to think positive thoughts for Dennis. So I stood outside in the cool night air and thanked God/Spirit that he was safe, that his friends Mitch and Robbie were also safe, that Carlye's life was coming together, that Riley was happy out West, that Cheryl and I both had our health, and that as a family, we felt things deeply. Before returning to bed, I told myself that I truly believed that some good news would come of Dennis.

Less than an hour later, the phone rang. I didn't even jump when it rang at that hour. I was convinced that regardless of the early hour, this call would only be positive—and it was. It was Riley.

"Turn on your computer," Riley exclaimed. "Dennis's picture is all over the web. Go to any major Canadian news site." I ran downstairs to my computer while Riley continued to explain. "Dennis is helping to carry one of the caskets at the ramp ceremony."

Sure enough. There was our tear-stained son wearing his anguish on his face. He was where he was supposed to be. Fortunately for Dennis's mental well-being, a padre in the Armed Forces had spoken up on behalf of Dennis and another friend, convincing authorities to allow these young men the right to attend the ramp ceremony—to grieve as humans. Dennis would be forever touched by this compassionate act of humanity, a strong indication of Christianity during that desperate time.

Cheryl and I held each other as we looked at the picture and read the various commentaries. Eventually, we said goodbye to Riley, retraced our steps upstairs, and, before shutting off my bed light, I took a few minutes to write out my daily gratitudes.

In August, Dennis returned home with all the symptoms of post-traumatic stress disorder and a family ring worn smooth by the joining desert forces of wind and sand. It was soon obvious that the Canadian Armed Forces were ill-equipped to face the magnitude of PTSD that was arriving back on base. Shocked and feeling misplaced, Dennis also returned home to a broken relationship with his girlfriend.

The doctors questioned if Dennis was suicidal. He was depressed and drinking far too much. The psychologist assigned to him thought that given his state, the betrayal by his girlfriend alone might be enough to push my son over the edge. Dennis was back in Gagetown but now on his own. It was a time of constant worry for the family. Then, much to his mother's worry, for she felt it was much too soon, Dennis began to date.

Six months later, Dennis was doing much better. He called me one night and shared that he did not wish his former girlfriend any ill will—actually quite the opposite—and he did not want his family holding any ill will against her either.

"I'm the one who was hurt, and if I can forgive, so should everyone else."

Dennis proceeded to explain that things had already started to improve in his life.

"We weren't ready, which was obvious, but that doesn't make her evil."

Not once did I ever hear Dennis express any overt anger at Muslims or the people of Afghanistan. The Taliban was the enemy. He knew that this minority group did not represent the majority of the others. Afghanistan had taught Dennis many lessons on many varying levels; no lesson was greater than what he learned about forgiveness. His experience also taught or at least reinforced many principles in my own life.

In November of 2008, I travelled alone to Victoria, BC, to visit with Riley and to watch two weekends of his rugby. It was ten days of relaxation, meeting lots of good people, and spending a lot of time in West Coast nature. Riley worked during the day, and a friend of Riley's, Gordon, was kind enough to lend me his truck for the week. On my previous trip to Victoria, a group of us had hiked Mount Finlayson, and I was anxious to do the 410-metre hike again, but this time on my own.

The morning that I had set aside for my hike was wet and dreary. The forecast did not sound promising. Regardless, I made the decision to drive the fourteen kilometres to Goldstream Park. Riley had told me that the place was known for its annual salmon run and the large number of bald eagles that this activity attracted, so I felt assured that regardless of the hike there would be lots to see.

It was raining when I reached the base of the mountain and had been for some time. Near the foot of the mountain, I met two lads a bit younger than I who had turned back halfway because of the questionable conditions. One of the guys had slipped on the wet footing and had twisted his ankle. The hike is a difficult one, steep in parts, and there are times where you need to use your hands on the rocky sections. I had good boots and was in good enough shape, so I continued on in spite of their well-meaning warning. Within minutes I came across another hiker; he was a much older gentleman. From above, he had overheard parts of my earlier conversation.

"Carry on," the man said, waving me forward without even stopping to chat. "Take your time, lad, be careful, and you'll do fine. I bet you it clears by the time you reach the top."

I smiled and gave him a thumbs up.

"Enjoy" was all he said, and he continued on his way as if there really was no other option for discussion.

Given the conditions, the hike was treacherous in parts. But I was enjoying the challenge. At halfway, the clouds appeared to be moving off. I took this as a good sign and carried onwards. As I reached the summit, the sky had cleared. I spied a young couple standing under a tree off the beaten path. Noticing my presence, the man approached me, holding his right index finger up against his lips.

When he was close enough for me to hear, he whispered, "You won't believe this when you see it." Then he turned and motioned me to follow him. After walking a short piece, he paused and pointed to the sky. There were about thirty eagles circling in the sky; it appeared to be a combination of parents and offspring. I stood there mesmerized by their beauty and grace. The couple eventually bid me goodbye to begin their descent, and I took a seat on some rocks and remained alone in the company of the eagles for close to an hour. I had never witnessed such natural beauty.

Back at the base of the mountain, I ran into a park employee and enthusiastically shared what I had just experienced. She said that it was likely a communal gathering, the salmon spawning grounds providing an opportunity for the juveniles to practice their ability to fly and to watch their elders to learn how food is caught.

"It's not a common occurrence at the park. I've never heard anyone share it," she said. "You are very fortunate," she added.

"I feel fortunate to have witnessed such a beautiful event."

"I don't expect to witness anything like it in my lifetime."

I could have turned back because of the weather or the two young men's warning. Instead, I worked through my obstacles, taking these impediments as a challenge. I was encouraged by the passion of the elderly man. I listened to my heart and was powerfully rewarded. On the summit of Mount Finlayson, in the company of many eagles, I felt truly blessed. It was the classic peak experience. That intense feeling of wonder and grace stayed with me for ages.

When Dennis met Holly, she already had a daughter, Shelby, age five, and I immediately fell in love with her. The following year I took her along with Cheryl and me to the Dominican Republic. One morning a British woman approached me. She and her daughter were travelling alone and she had been bothered by a local man who was already drinking heavily. She said, "I saw this man talking to Shelby and her little friends, leaving alcoholic drinks with them while he swam in the pool." When I confronted the man, he denied the allegations, but then made light of me to his friends as I turned to leave. I lost it. He backed down.

Afterwards, in the company of staff, he tracked me down. He told me, "I have never in all my life experienced anyone so angry. Your eyes told me that you would kill me."

He was right.

In the days, weeks, and months that followed, in the serene rural surroundings of my home in St. Catherines, I found myself easily frustrated and much too prone to states of anger. That single event during my holiday had triggered something deeper; I had to accept that I had unresolved issues. That experience taught me that I was still consumed with rage towards my father and the allegations.

Then that spring, the Catholic Church in Ireland was devastated by the knowledge that several allegations against nineteen priests between 1996 and 2009 had been covered up by authorities within the Church. The media could not write enough. Allegations would soon surface in Sweden and then spread across a half-dozen countries including the United States and the Pope's native Germany. On CNN, photographs of priests being taken from their parish homes or being led into courthouses continually flashed. The Vatican would declare this state of affairs as a "global crisis."

Left unresolved, the patterns in my life, patterns in everyone's life, keep repeating.

Monday, December 7, 2009
St. Catherines

Moody Dog, Bridget, and myself had our first winter walk of the season. The snow-covered trees were beautiful. I had a major insight. I realized that more than anything else, I would like everyone to feel as good as I did at that very moment, surrounded by the beauty of snow, nature, and my dogs.

But a few years ago, before I accepted counselling, when I lived alone, I had been willing to love everyone to that same level with the exception of myself. Shame does that to you.

Part IX

One cannot live in the afternoon of life according to the program of life's morning; for what was great in the morning will be of little importance in the evening, and what in the morning was true will at evening have become a lie.

Carl Jung

Test everything; hold fast what is good.

1 Thessalonians 5:21

CARL JUNG WROTE ABOUT how "life's morning program" is often of little importance or even fact "by the evening of our lives." He used the phrase "the two halves of life" to acknowledge the two clear steps to human and spiritual development. I was reintroduced to the wisdom of Carl Jung through the writing of the Franciscan priest, Fr. Richard Rohr, most notably in his book *Falling Upwards: A Spirituality for the Two Halves of Life*, in which Rohr writes beautifully of how the failings of our first half of life—our heartbreaks, our disappointments—"are actually stepping stones to the spiritual joys" of our second half of life.

In 2011, I was turning fifty and was definitely entering or living the second half of my life. I was about to embark on another challenging stage in my reluctant quest for spiritual truths. I had learned much in the first half of my life, but there was still room for a tremendous amount of spiritual growth. This next chapter in my journey was very much shaped by a serious relapse in my health condition. I came into contact with some air-quality issues from water-related damage at my new workplace, which overpowered my immune system that had already been compromised by my old workplace. All the same old symptoms returned. My body was speaking for me again.

There was also the reality that my father had died from a brain tumour in his fifties.

I told myself that I was more than my father's history.

It could have been so easy just to give in. Fortunately, I had overcome a significant health challenge once before, but now my faith was even more grounded in my spiritual beliefs and past experiences. I believed that I would get better again. I continued to believe that life would get better. This time round I was going to trust, listen, and learn from my intuition, dreams, and synchronicities. Life still had its challenges, but those spiritual experiences were a blessing.

Shelby had a break from school and was staying with Cheryl and me for a few extra days. As usual, she had fallen asleep in our bed. I had gotten up to get ready for work and was trying extra hard to be quiet so as not to wake her. I was about to leave the kitchen area when who appeared but my pyjama-clad granddaughter, with eyes half closed and bed hair.

"What are you doing up?" I asked.

Shelby just held her ground. "Are you okay, Grampy?"

I knelt down before her in my suit and tie and took her small hands in mine. "I'm fine, love," I tried to assure her. "Why do you ask?"

"You're not fun anymore."

I was lost for words. I thought I had been doing better, much better this time round, but I was only fooling myself. After being off work for close to a month, I was back there again, but work was killing me. Every ounce of energy I had went into showing up for work.

"You don't take me for walks or go to the park like we used to. You're not happy."

I took Shelby in my arms and carried her back upstairs and tucked her into bed.

"I'm going to get happy, love. I promise you. Now go back to sleep." I tucked the blankets in about her and kissed her forehead. "Thank you, for caring."

It took the honesty, innocence, and compassion of an eight-year-old child to break down my walls. My wife, my children, my closest relatives had all shared their concerns, but this spirited child had broken through to me. She was absolutely right. I wasn't happy; I was no fun; I wasn't spending quality time with my granddaughter or anyone else outside of work.

It was the initiative I needed. Our roles, though briefly, had been reversed. I allowed myself to learn from this beautiful child. My mind was racing. I drove to work that morning and told my employers I was going to see my family doctor, that I needed to take some extended time off work—I didn't think they would take the word of my granddaughter.

People would often remark how fortunate Shelby was to have a grandparent who spent so much time with her, but I have always answered that Shelby came into my life when I needed her most; I believe we both needed each other. She was another of God/Spirit's blessings.

I was scared.

It was during my early transition back to work, and I had left one school in the late afternoon and was now driving to West Kent

Elementary for an after-school meeting. A few years prior, I had actually worked out of this very school when the water pipes broke at our office building and we experienced serious flooding and water damage. I had also rented a nearby apartment for a few years in the early nineties; I knew the area well.

This had the appearance of a normal day, but while driving, I lost all sense of direction and was unable to find my way to the school. I was completely overwhelmed. The area I am speaking about compromises a few blocks. It's not a big city; there was no major traffic. Still, I literally had to turn around, get back on the main road and come in from a different direction. I was certain that I was losing my mind.

I said nothing at the meeting. I admit I wasn't mentally present; I simply went through the motions. Back at home, I was physically and emotionally drained and exhausted. I shared with Cheryl what had happened.

Cheryl sensed what I was feeling. "It's not in your head," she assured me.

My wife gave me the courage to hang in there. Sometimes, we just need to know that someone truly cares.

In *The Jesuit Guide to Almost Everything*, Father James Martin shares how an illness changed him, and how God was there. And while he may have been grateful afterwards for the experience, he is open enough to admit that he wasn't happy about the situation, and nor would he have chosen it; he certainly wanted the illness taken away. And he never completely understood the situation while he was living it. He has reasoned that it was not that God wanted him to be sick, but, rather, when his defenses were down, he was able to see things more clearly.

I would never suggest that we seek out illness or danger or crisis.

But when we are broken, we must seek out meaning and view the interconnection of this world. Suffering can only have any meaning when we transcend the actual pain. The meaning is when we increase our capacity to love and to be loved.

The question for me was given my situation, how might God/ Spirit be brought to light?

Former Franciscan priest Brendan Manning is the best-selling author of *The Ragamuffin Gospel.* He has another book, which I love, entitled *The Furious Longing of God.* In the book, Manning quotes Dom Verner Moore, who writes of the beauty of a "quasi-experiential realization of the warmth and tenderness of God's love."

Manning calls this "baptism by fire," which "can happen in weekly worship, by hearing Scripture, in shared prayer, even by holding an infant." This experience is available to anyone who desires "to move beyond theoretical abstractions to living experience, intensely real."

On February 18, 2011, Declan Slade MacKenzie was born. And a new level of spirituality was created within me.

Five months later, the summer sun was warm on our front deck. There was a stillness to Dennis that I hadn't seen in ages, a tranquility where once stood only restlessness and agitation. He had recently taken parental leave from the army to care for his son. He was fully devoted to the well-being of this child who was now resting on my lap. The birth of Declan was a welcome distraction for him, and it physically removed him from the army surroundings. He and I were enjoying a drink, sunshine, and conversation.

"How's the counselling going?" I asked.

"Excellent. The psychologist is a wonderful man. You would really like him. I hope that you get to meet him some day."

"That would be nice."

Declan squirmed, so we paused in our conversation to watch the child.

Then Dennis began again, picking up where we had left off.

"The psychologist is doing great work, and I'm still taking my medication… but for all the therapies that I have received, you're holding the best treatment for my PTSD."

Giving of himself to care for another living being, a vulnerable, trusting soul, provided Dennis with an opportunity, at least intermittently, to move beyond his own worries. Giving unconditional love, he received unconditional love. Interestingly enough, Declan was having the same impact on me.

Without any knowledge of Dennis's and my conversation, within days, Cheryl started to refer to Declan as "Grampy's medicine." It was obvious to everyone that I felt better in the child's presence: lighter, less anxious, and less stressed. I didn't waste time dwelling on myself. The impact that this child was having on Dennis and me was therapeutic and healing.

In *Accidental Saints*, minister Nadia Bolz-Weber shares the power of holding a child during a dark time. I could relate. Bolz-Weber came to refer to that experience as "the baby of life, the holding of which is for the healing of the people." She adds, "Because the holy things we need for healing and sustenance are almost the same as the ordinary things right in front of us." This was so true. What truly mattered most was our perception.

I had never been in a father's role with babies. It was a soulful pleasure I had been denied. The experience of sleeping with Declan was so gratifying. I found such beauty and contentment in the four-thirty mornings, getting a bottle for the child, and taking him back to bed. No book, no lecture could ever match the power of that experience. There is no grander verification that the source of life is an intelligence far greater than us, and that all of humanity is intrinsically connected, than looking into the eyes of a child.

Grampy's medicine. It made me recall a dream back on Labour Day in 1998, the first time I dreamt of Mom after she died. In my dream, Father was with her and there was a third person in the backseat. The dream ended when she introduced me to a child, a fair-haired boy. Declan was the first fair-haired child to come into my life.

It was a particularly warm morning for the end of August, and Shelby and I had taken the day to spend together at Brackley Beach on the beautiful north shore of Prince Edward Island. As I was driving along, Shelby, now eight, had an "aha" moment. While looking out the window at the passing countryside, deep in thought, Shelby turned to me and asked, "Why did I trust you when I met you?"

It was a fair question.

Shelby proceeded to explain. "I really didn't know you. I didn't grow up with you. Mom didn't know you. I didn't fall to sleep watching videos with my other grampies."

"I'm not sure, Shelby. I don't know why you felt that way."

I continued to drive out towards the beach when, once again, without any fear of judgement or rejection, Shelby openly shared her thoughts. "The first time I met you," she said, "I knew you would do anything for me." Then she added, "And I don't mean buy me things."

Then as if this was our normal everyday conversation, Shelby began to once again talk about her favourite beach and shared everything that she planned to accomplish: swimming, sand castles, and then ice cream on the way home.

Children are not born with religion, but they are born with an innate intuitive awareness. There is great insight in children. And great innocence. Their minds and hearts are open. We all come into the world this way with a pure connection to our higher energy, be it God/Spirit or the universe. Religion is a human convention, while consciousness and intuitive awareness is a natural law. It is our world of logical, structured conformity that blocks this innate awareness. There is a tendency among people to get wrapped up or lost in the status quo thinking. We stop listening to ourselves for fear we might be wrong or judged as being wrong; we adapt to our surroundings.

I hope that Shelby never loses the wonder and innocence of childhood, that it never fades away. I never want her magic to die. I hope that she always sees the beauty in this life that she once saw and shared as a child. Or having temporarily lost it, she reclaims its miracle as readily as possible.

The first vinyl record album I ever bought was Elton John's *Greatest Hits*—his original collection. I was thirteen years old, visiting Toronto for the first time with my family. The album held great significance on many levels. On the cover, Elton John was dressed in a white suit, wearing a white fedora and his trademark extra-large sunglasses. He was sitting sideways in front of his piano. Given my age, I very likely bought the album for the song "Crocodile Rock," but his classic ballads like "Daniel" and "Your Song" soon became my favourites.

On September 14, 2011, Elton John came to the sleepy little town of Summerside, PEI. There wasn't a chance I was going to miss it. Cheryl, her sister, and I went to the show. Inside, I was thirteen again.

His music resonated through to my core. I felt so alive. My childhood legend played a slightly different version of "Rocket Man (I think it's Going be a Long, Long Time)," and, in the darkened stadium, tears began to run down my cheeks. I was truly allowing myself to feel, deeper than I had in years. Maybe it was going to be a long, long time, but I knew that I was on the right track.

Being so moved at that concert was the breakthrough that Dr. John F. Demartini writes about in *The Breakthrough Experience*: "There's an immortal part of us that knows the truth and a mortal part that denies it." He writes about those times when we have read or listened to something that brings us to tears; these are gifts, he says, from the immortal part. Not all gifts come in the most traditional of settings.

The following workweek ended with a late phone call from an emotional parent. I could hear her verbally abusive husband cursing in the background. Damaged people damaging others. I understood mental illness and could generally leave this at work, but I told myself my time was up—I didn't have the energy any longer. The negativity was draining what little energy I had left. It wasn't fair to my staff or the families. I was going to devote myself to more positive energy.

It was time to put more loving thoughts into concrete action.

Later that month, Cheryl and her sister started making natural Christmas wreaths and preservatives as gifts; they called their business "Muckle Innis." I knew this endeavour would be another healthy wholesome outlet.

Home alone one day, I went out to our small barn and cleaned it up for Muckle Innis. I found some old-fashioned Christmas lights with the larger bulbs and hung them along the inside ceiling. Then I located an old CD player and got out some Christmas music. I had the place looking pretty neat and cosy for the ladies.

The following afternoon, I took Bridget and Rugby to the woods in Tracy's truck and cut fresh greenery for the wreaths: pine and flat spruce branches. It was a beautiful warm winter afternoon: 10 degrees Celsius and sunshine. We had a fabulous time in the woods. The girls called me their "wreath monkey."

That evening we had a ball. I cut up the boughs, and Cheryl and Tracy did the creative work. Christmas music was playing in the background, the lights giving a soulful cast, the dogs lying on the dog beds I had taken out to the barn. It was a Christmas-wreath factory, and we loved it. The wreaths were works of art.

The girls lasted much longer than I did. Outside it started to rain ever so lightly. I excused myself and went into the house and had a late, hot shower. Afterwards, I stood outside under the veranda, wearing my flannel Johnny shirt, rubber boots, and a stocking cap. I absolutely loved standing there looking out at the barn—all lit up at night, greenery lying about outside, Bridget sleeping on the ramp into the double doors. It just felt right.

On Tuesday, December 6, 2011, I decided to travel to Charters Settlement, outside of Fredericton, to spend some time visiting with Dennis and his family, to hang out with the grandchildren. My car had Bluetooth but was not voice-activated, so while I drove, especially if I was alone, it was a common practice to rest my cell phone in one of the cup holders to allow for easy access. On the afternoon in question, as I was approaching Salisbury, I had a strong intuition or a premonition that I should drive with my cell phone on my body.

Why? I asked.

The message I received was *Because if I was unfortunate enough to be in an accident, my phone would be thrown around in the car, and I would be unable to call Cheryl for help.*

For anyone familiar with that area, you will know that Salisbury Irving is one of the few rest stops along the double highway between Moncton and Fredericton and, as a result, is a common and welcomed "truck stop." When I ordered my coffee, my cell phone was still staring at me from the console. It would have been so easy to discount and ignore this sort of thing. But I grabbed my phone and put it into my front pocket before pulling out onto the divided highway.

At around 3:50, Dennis called. I explained that I was still outside of the village of Oromocto, and, according to a recent mileage sign, I would likely be arriving in Charters Settlement around 4:30. I hung up and continued along my way. To break up the boredom, I put in a CD of Coldplay, skipped ahead to the title track, "Viva la Vida," and listened to the instrumental intro. The road signs told me that I was approaching Oromocto and Camp Gagetown.

Then I lost awareness while driving.

I did not fall asleep or blank out but became completely dissociated. The next thing that I was conscious of was driving up a hill, passing a car that seemed to have come out of nowhere, and a different song was playing. In the rearview mirror I noticed a truck coming up too fast, but there was nowhere to pull over on the outside lane. I began to sweat profusely. Fortunately, I calmed myself and picked up enough speed to overtake the neighbouring car, pulled back into the slow lane, let the approaching truck pass, and waited until there was a safe place to pull over on the shoulder of the road. Then my nose began to bleed. I checked my pocket and patted my cell phone.

I looked down at the clock and couldn't believe that I had miscalculated my arrival time so poorly, as it was already 4:15 and I had not reached Oromocto yet.

Easing back on the highway, I drove on and welcomed what

I thought was the billboard of the solider welcoming drivers to Oromocto. But I was dead wrong; instead, the sign was that of the Mountie welcoming people to the capital city of Fredericton. I was not sure how long I had lost awareness, but I had bypassed the entire highway section of Camp Gagetown and Oromocto. I was so grateful that there was no accident. I got to my son's place at 4:28, as I had predicted.

I told myself that I was never going to ignore my intuition again.

The following day I was having another nosebleed, so I had myself checked out at the local emergency room. They were quite concerned about my story. I had a bad headache and was really flushed, so they checked my vitals right away. My blood pressure was extremely high: 198 over something in the 90s. Had it been 200, they would have had to hospitalize me. Given my experience, the nurse said I was extremely lucky to be alive. Bloodwork showed too many irregularities for me to drive home and further tests were ordered. The Oromocto medical staff was thorough and amazing. They made a referral for me to see a neurologist and have an MRI back on the Island.

I am extremely pleased that this is where this portion of the story ends. I did not cause a serious or fatal accident while driving my car. I did not need my cell phone, but I would have had it on me in such an event. Some readers will believe the message I received was no more than a random thought, and its existence at that very time no more than chance or a coincidence. Previously I, too, would have been quite comfortable to accept that line of reasoning; however, as a result of too many profound experiences, the distance from where I view premonitions and unexplained communications has changed. Many of my experiences may not be easily explained, but I can assure you that they are true.

It was early December; winter was coming. I was living in the country. A CT scan did not find a brain tumour or blood clots. Still, something had taken place, and there were irregularities in my bloodwork. The neurologist took my license for four months. It wasn't an overly happy time.

Friday, December 30, 2011
St. Catherines

I had a beautiful dream last night. It had to do with a brain scan and a conversation I was having with a doctor about "bucket wishes." I explained to the doctor that I had just completed a major bucket at Christmas when I offered tickets down south to Cheryl and her sister for a holiday together. As the doctor was hooking me up to the brain scan, he told me that the process would bring to mind other bucket wishes.

Once I went into a trance, silhouette images of Shelby appeared on the screen. She was snowboarding, dancing, hiking, graduating from high school, and so forth. The images just kept coming and repeating.

In the book jacket of Fr. Richard Rohr's book *Falling Upwards: A Spirituality for the Two Halves of Life*, Rohr acknowledges that some people "grow spiritually more by doing it wrong than by doing it right," and that "those who have fallen, failed, or gone down are the only ones who understand up." While our addictions, illnesses, and failures may seem like "a huge price to pay," nothing less breaks down our false selves and opens us to love.

My brother's life had been falling apart, and I hadn't known it. It was the start of a new year. He knew that he needed change. He came to my house and told me that he was an alcoholic and had been suffering from severe depression for years. I couldn't help but wonder what would have happened if his depression had gotten worse and he hadn't reached out for help. What if it all had become too much?

In my mind, I revisited my maternal uncle's suicide attempt. The day he jumped from the Charlottetown wharf, and I went to his apartment looking for a note—the emptiness of his apartment... the lack of life... how I couldn't breathe. And then my mother's reaction, apologizing for bothering me, and then the questioning: Why? How could he have been so unhappy? Why hadn't he asked for help?

I didn't want these cycles to keep repeating. I wanted things to change. We could write a different ending.

It was January 18, 2012, the day my brother admitted that his life was falling apart. Hayden was fifty-three, in the second half of his life, and in his eyes, he had failed—but he didn't quit. He decided that day to make all the right changes. He understood falling upwards.

The next day I accompanied him when he went to see his family doctor. The doctor and nurse were so empathic and understanding about the situation. The nurse shared her own earlier struggles with depression. When Hayden opened up to support, it was readily given. These people were exactly what he needed. I sat to the side and listened while my brother sounded like a stranger, sharing the darkest aspects of his depression to which I had been totally oblivious. Sure, I wasn't blind to his drinking; I had had concerns for many years about how his moods would change while he drank and become darker the following day. But I was unaware of the severity.

Hayden quit drinking, he saved his marriage, he found a good counsellor, and he started writing more (he had been a journalist in an earlier career). He had found new hope. He continued to check in on me most days, and I, in turn, would ask him how he was doing. If Cheryl was busy, my brother drove me to my appointments. I believe we were good for each other—real brothers. I was so proud of how he was transforming. Though he never once talked of God or Divine Intervention or of his own divinity, I believed spirit was working through him. My brother was a good spiritual inspiration, whether he knew it or not.

The next major breakthrough for my overall health was yet another example of synchronicity. My family doctor admitted that he didn't have the answers, but, more importantly, he sought out second opinions. He made a referral to the Nova Scotia Environmental Health Centre (presently known as the Integrated Chronic Care Service clinic) in Fall River, Nova Scotia. I was very fortunate that my doctor had done some of his medical placement at this unconventional site.

In January of 2012, Fall River took me on as an out-of-province patient. The clinic is research-oriented and is affiliated with Dalhousie University in Halifax and a research-based hospital in Texas, the largest environmental clinic in North America. For the first time in my health journey that had spanned a decade, it felt as if someone wholly understood my condition. The doctor I was assigned to was extremely knowledgeable and empathic; he was intelligence and compassion in action. In February, I spent a week at their day clinic.

The medical staff asked a lot from me, physically and emotionally. The underlying question was always, "So how much do you sincerely desire to be well?" This was key. For it emphasized the importance of intent: wherever we place our attention gets our energy. I was never asked to take responsibility for the workplace conditions, just to take responsibility for all the factors that I rightfully owned. It was so easy to focus on the chemicals alone, to have that perfect outlet for blame and my anger. But, if I wanted to heal, that limiting attitude had to change. That was my responsibility. The best health advice I was ever given was to be an active participant in my healing. And this rule applied to all domains of healing—physical, emotional, mental, and spiritual—and while the four appear as separate entities, they are intertwined on many levels as one. It only made sense that our health and wellness are dependent on the alignment of all four.

Our emotional issues or blockages do not necessarily cause illness, but they weaken our immune system, which makes us more susceptible to illness, and they directly impact our healing process. Denying my issues taxed my system, helping to make me more susceptible to illness. However, I believed that this same sensitive, intuitive nature could awaken healing energies if I was open to accepting and using this energy.

Under this holistic approach, it felt like the staff was asking me, "What does your body need to heal itself?" It was as if they believed that only I could know the answer, that deep inside I did know the answer, if I would only listen to myself and then live it—and that everyone had this ability. I had never ever been approached like this. It was reinvigorating.

Back in St. Catherines, the early stages of the new lifestyle regime didn't go so well. It was a lot to absorb; it felt overwhelming. I had to give up so many things: coffee, chocolate, fried foods, diet Coke, preservatives, and most alcohol. There were other restrictions as well: I had to exercise daily but in moderation, no television or electrical stimulation an hour before bed, definitely no television in the bedroom. And bedtime was ten o'clock. I had to give up control. Regardless of how good these recommendations were for me and the degree to which I was willing to follow them, I thoroughly resented what felt like a lack of autonomy.

Many nights I would bid goodnight to Cheryl and often guests and head to bed at my appointed time. One night as I was heading upstairs to bed, I felt like literally stomping on each individual, cursed step. I got to the top of the stairs, stood on the landing, and took a deep breath. All I could think of was my mild-mannered mother battling cancer and wanting to take her bedsheets in her hands and rip them to shreds. I actually laughed at myself.

Illness and disease can change our experiences; they can change how we relate to the world around us. I had been exposed to chemicals, and my central nervous system and immune system had been compromised. I could not continue to interrelate to people the same way; and, for the most part, I was beginning to see the world differently. One perspective wasn't better or worse, just different; however, I could relate to some people more openly and honestly than others.

Life couldn't remain the same, but it didn't have to be meaningless.

Father's Day, 2012.

I took Declan upstairs with me; he was supposed to be going for a nap. Instead, he was bouncing on my stomach while I lay in bed. Downstairs, Shelby heard her little brother's laughter, so she came up to join us. Now the two grandchildren were having a great time on my bed.

Then in the midst of the laughter and play, Shelby paused to look very seriously at her brother. She stared for a brief spell before turning her attention to me.

"You are going to be Declan's person," Shelby said.

"Why do you say that, Shelby?"

"When I was young, before I even knew you or Nanny, I always had my grandmother, Dad's mom. She's who I went to when Dad was angry. She was always there for me."

"That was nice that you had her in your life."

"Declan will always need you. It's a good thing."

Accepting life for what it is does not mean that we have to blindly accept any harmful or unfair actions; in reality, it is the complete opposite. Once you truly accept what is, and stop trying to control the situation, then you will naturally find the freedom to act out of love for others and yourself. Unobstructed, love is our primary emotion.

As soon as I began to empower myself, my anger slowly began to soften.

There was another paradox at play: a major part of empower-ment for me was allowing myself to admit I needed help and then to actually ask for the help. I was used to being in the role of the one giving guidance, not the one receiving it. In my ignorance, I had convinced myself that it was about strength and confidence and independence, but the truth was, once again, that I was fearful. I feared being vulnerable, looking weak, or being rejected. This insistence of having a strong self-image was paramount. I had strengths and skills in many areas, but I was weak and frail in others. Asking for help was the complete opposite sensation of feeling victimized, and that was crucial for me. In the end, I did not feel helpless, needy, or dependent; I felt supported and guided. Accepting help from others didn't make me less of a person; it actually made me more whole. I had to get rid of my old way of thinking; I still had to unlearn a few things.

It is often said that true growth only occurs when we overcome resistance. I had made a commitment to heal. As a result, the tipping point for me in my health journey occurred in the summer of 2012 when I made a conscious decision to file a complaint against my workplace with the Human Rights Commission. I had asked for work accommodations and it just wasn't happening. Both parties, the school board and myself, were going in circles, and my mental and physical well-being were continuing to suffer. I knew that my nervous system was being deeply influenced by my anger, stress, and other emotions. My immediate decision to take charge of my situation was the healthiest action I could take.

The staff at the Integrated Chronic Care Service clinic was instrumental, with their support and insights, in my decision to go to Human Rights. Their approach was not judgemental or accusatory; it was totally about education, awareness, and work culture. The executive director and his staff at Human Rights were models of humanity and professionalism. The lawyer I was given the right to hire was brilliant. I was introduced to the Canadian Association of Workers' Advisors and Advocates and here I met yet another wonderful, talented lawyer who helped me appeal the Workers' Compensation decision. My former superintendent was a godsend, and now in the role of minister of education, he refused to treat me as a mere disgruntled employee. All of these great people came into my life once I opened the door… once I got over myself and asked for help and was receptive to their guidance and wisdom.

Then gratitude took on an entirely new level of awareness.

In addition to the professional help, Cheryl continued to be just as amazing. Because of my brain fog and the ensuing risk of misinterpretation and forgetfulness, she attended all initial meetings with my family doctor, the neurologist, my lawyer, and Human Rights. She researched and found a yoga instructor who just happened to be holding classes out in the country, not far from us, in an older renovated community hall. Cheryl also researched my new diet restrictions and cooked accordingly. My brother continued his supporting role and even drove me to Halifax for a medical appointment.

But it was more than that.

Good people surrounded me, and just being in their presence was healing. Friends and extended family called and checked in periodically to see how I was doing. Staff members sent emails. My cousin Michelle was especially mindful, and godchildren kept in close touch. My friend Bob made sure to take me out for an occasional beer and a bite to eat. Another friend, Alan, and I would take in the odd movie. Marcel and Mark checked in on me weekly. These were wonderful people. I felt loved, and the truth was that I wasn't that much fun to be around. But these people did not abandon me; they kept showing up.

In the book *Accidental Saint* by Lutheran minister Nadia Bolz-Weber is an inspiring chapter entitled "You Are Not 'The Blessing.'" I believe Bolz-Weber when she wrote that "Christ's presence is not embodied in those who feed the hungry (as important as that work is), but Christ's presence is in the hungry being fed." That's a powerful concept. She proceeds to clarify that "Christ does not come to us *as* the poor and hungry," but that Christ comes to us in the *needs* being met—that "holy place where we meet others' needs and have our needs met."

That is an extremely relevant and important point.

Bolz-Weber is not one to mince words. "No one gets to play Jesus," she writes. "We are all the needy and the ones who meet needs. To place ourselves or anyone else in only one category is to lie to ourselves."

Theologian Henri J. M. Nouwen complements this view when he writes, "Our brokenness may appear beautiful, but our brokenness has no other beauty but the beauty that comes from the compassion that surrounds it."

The helping is as meaningful as the cure.

As I reflected on these two pastoral authors, I went back to the Bible and reread the passage where Jesus heals the blind man (St. John 9:2). According to the passage, as Jesus and a disciple pass by a blind man, the disciple asks who did sin, the man or his parents whose actions would cause the blindness. "Jesus answered, 'neither hath this man sinned, nor his parents: but that the works of God should be manifest in him.'"

There is nothing spiritual about putting up walls. There is nothing spiritual about suffering. There is nothing spiritual about refusing to let good people in. Love isn't an isolating event. Spirituality is in the acts of caring. Community is always a part of healing.

In my life, I was both the needy and the one who met needs. It was time for me to be humble and honest.

My doctor put me off work, again. This routine was getting old. I woke up one morning feeling extremely anxious. Before my feet even touched the floor, I knew something was off. Downstairs, I ignored breakfast and went straight to my office and checked my work emails. There was my name in print as an agenda item on Monday morning's management meeting. It didn't sit right; my guts began to tighten.

All morning my mind was preoccupied with the agenda for a meeting I wasn't going to. After lunch, I left the house to run a few errands. It was well after one o'clock before I reached the post office and had to wait in line for a parcel. On the way home I had an anxiety attack. This was new for me. I was so overwhelmed that I had to pull over to the shoulder of the road, collect myself, and just breathe. Arriving home, there was a missed call and message recorded on the phone at 1:37. It was from the new superintendent about returning to work.

The following morning, I got out a book called *Transforming Anxiety*, by Doc Childre and Debrorah Rozman, which I had bought at the Fall River Clinic. The chapter where my bookmark rested dealt with being overwhelmed and anxious at work. The main premise was to look at "significance." The authors were convinced that any serious reflective thought would clearly show how work issues are not truly significant—not in your present life and certainly not from a spiritual dimension. It also encouraged looking at ingrained beliefs associated with work. The closing message of the chapter was that we all need to take full responsibility for how we allow our beliefs to drive us. We, and we alone, are responsible for acknowledging the true significance of work in our lives. The timing and relevance of this reading couldn't have been more perfect.

One morning following a very deep sleep, I literally woke to a communication of three words: "Doctor, Dyer, and Memes." It was so apparent that this message was significant that I took the pad and pen from my bedside nightstand and wrote down the three words: *Doctor, Dyer, and Memes*. At the time, these three words together held absolutely no meaning for me. I proceeded to get up, dress, and stuff the piece of paper into my jeans pocket.

It was a Saturday, and Cheryl was home. I made some breakfast, but my energy was very low that day—Cheryl could easily tell my state by the look of my glassy eyes.

"Not a good day?" Cheryl asked, but it was really just an ac-knowledgement.

"Not a good day," I answered.

I had only been out of bed an hour at most, but I was already grabbing a blanket and heading for the couch to watch the morning news, an exasperating routine. Nothing was catching my attention, so I ended up flicking aimlessly through the channels. Eventually, I came to a public broadcasting station out of Detroit, Michigan, a channel that I had never watched and didn't know existed. On the television screen was a gentleman I didn't recognize giving a lecture. His name was Dr. Wayne Dyer.

"Cheryl, can you come over here?"

I took the sheet of paper from my pocket and passed it to my wife. Three simple words, "Doctor, Dyer, and Memes."

"I know I have to listen to this," I said.

The topic at that very moment was "memes," also a term that I had never heard before. Dyer proceeded to describe memes as the viral, self-defeating thinking habits that prevent a person from living their life's dreams.

Now completely intrigued by the synchronicity, I continued to watch the show.

Dyer walked across a large stage, and these colourful signs began to appear above and about him, signs with written messages of what he believed were the most common memes. Some stood out more strongly than others, such as, "It's not in my nature," "I don't have the energy," and "It will be difficult." I could relate to all of those excuses. But the one that really hit home read, "There will be family drama." Bingo.

Family drama... would that be enough to sway me from living my life purposes?

It was another intense validation of my intuition I could not ignore. It was like what was truly important to me would be revealed when I was ready and if I remained open to the teachings.

I believed that what I needed to nurture me would in time come to me as well.

Gregg Braden, author of *The Spontaneous Healing of Belief*, believes that "changing our beliefs may be the most difficult thing that we do in life." Braden quotes Geoff Heath of the University of Derby in England, who writes, "To change our beliefs is to change our identities."

For many people, programmed beliefs eventually can become defined as our truths, and we want to remain loyal to our stories. Look how poorly so many do with separation and retirement: when they feel they have lost their identities, they feel invisible.

It was not that my former beliefs were false; they had served a purpose at one time. They just no longer served me.

I fell asleep after work. I was exhausted. I woke knowing that I needed some exercise. Cheryl had gone to Zumba classes. Outside, the high winds were blowing snow about. I put on a face mask, donned a headlamp, and took off with Rugby at eight o'clock. The winds threw me off at first, but the temperature was good.

Rugby and I walked through the backfields, then down along the river. We came to the spot where the water runs off the bank. In the middle of a landscape of white and wind was the sound of fresh running water, and grass still green where the adjacent snow had melted. The wind was extreme along the open stretch of river before the bridge, but it was heavenly when we turned around and the wind was at our backs.

On our return walk, we hiked up the hill beside our house,

then stood from on high and looked around. I love the look of our house in winter, nestled in nature's valley, so tranquil and warm-looking. Snow was piled up everywhere. Then I noticed the car lights. I was so excited to see Cheryl's car driving down our lane, knowing she was home.

Sometimes there is such beauty amidst life's hard conditions. Sometimes the peace is more meaningful among life's extremes. Sometimes we need the opposite to know what we value most.

The following night was cloudy with few stars out. Rugby was aging, but we still ventured out for a walk in the backwoods. On the way back, once again we made our way to the top of the neighbouring hill. While walking in darkness, a full moon with an orange cast broke through the dark clouds. Its beauty stopped me cold in my tracks.

Does everyone feel this way? I asked Rugby.

Later that night in bed, I picked up a book from my nightstand. The book included a quote that the Christian mystic and Romantic poet, William Blake, once wrote in a letter: "The tree which moves some to tears of joy is in the eyes of others only a green thing that stands in the way."

So I sat up in bed and questioned myself:

What could be wrong in finding such joy from simple pleasures as witnessing an orange moon?

What is wrong in finding wonderful company in an old aging dog?

What could be wrong in feeling a spiritual essence in an eagle, my neighbouring ducks, and all of nature and in everyone whom I meet?

What if these simple pleasures go against the grain—against the norms and conventional thinking? Would the rewards of conformity be worth it? Definitely not.

The first spiritual highlight of 2013 was the wedding of our daughter, Carlye, to her fiancé, Jon Burke. It was a great family event, and the activities actually started earlier in the spring, when I decided to have a "wedding barn" built in our backyard for the occasion. The rehearsal party was a success. The Burkes fed everyone. At one point in the evening, I was drinking expensive scotch that Carlye and Jon had bought for me, smoking a cigar, surrounded by young, beautiful people; Rugby was sleeping at my feet. I told myself, *Life doesn't get much better.*

My daughter's wedding was to take place outside. It rained that morning, and there was still a heavy mist by late afternoon. I felt confident that we could pull it off; we decided to take a chance. The rain stopped as I began to speak and started to rain lightly once again when the ceremony finished. We were so grateful.

There was a wonderful blending of people; the highlight of the night was yet to come. Carlye had become friends with a young man who had been seriously injured. He was now in a wheelchair. Two years ago, doctors believed he would be totally paralyzed. He was excited to be coming to the wedding, and he had promised Carlye he would dance with her. He had been practicing for this moment for months. When he stood to waltz with Carlye, there wasn't a dry eye in the barn. It was obvious to anyone present that this was pure spirituality in action.

The wedding was wonderful. Carlye said it best, "Nothing went right, and it was perfect."

The second spiritual highlight of that summer took place the first weekend in August, on the shore behind my childhood church.

Over the year, a new mom had approached me two or three times, wanting me to "baptize" her daughter. "It would be more of a celebration," she said, "non-religious, a welcoming."

My traditional religious beliefs were well ingrained.

"This feels like blasphemy," I told Cheryl. "It would be sacrilegious in the eyes of the community."

"What community? You're not doing a church blessing. Think of it as bathing the baby in seawater," she joked.

Once again, I had to challenge my limiting beliefs and expose them to inquiry.

I contacted the mother. "Would there be a big crowd?"

"I expect ten to twenty people. Mainly my family. A few close friends." Both parents' families lived in other provinces.

I worked on the celebration off and on for a few days. I actually quite enjoyed pulling it together: acknowledging the love of family, the supporting community, and the spiritual guardians. I focused on the power of a blessing that doesn't reside in its formality, but rather that is spoken from the heart. I found passages that spoke of the symbolism of the ocean and how beneath the waves, like water, we are all one. The maternal grandmother agreed to read a passage from the Bible. But most of all I focused on the child, and how she had become such a source of love and meaning and purpose for both of her parents, who were later in life starting a family. Mom thought she had resolved to living a life without children of her own. Then through her own admission, she felt something was missing. "There had to be more," she told me. The father always knew that his life would not be complete without being a father to a child of his own.

How could I not want to be part of this celebration?

On a beautiful sunny Saturday morning in August, Cheryl and I drove out to that strip of sandbar located at the end of a dirt road well back behind the church. By the time we started, there were over fifty people in attendance. I just looked at Cheryl, shook my head, and mouthed the words *Oh, well*. It proved to be a beautiful day.

I began by taking my first steps towards representing myself with my Human Rights case. My lawyer had done excellent work. He had taken me quite far, but now the school board was stalling. It was now costing me a lot of money, and I had no job security. It was time for me to take a stand at a higher level. I contacted the board lawyer and requested a meeting.

That's when I noticed a paradox.

I had an invisible illness. Yet the more work-related personnel showed a sense of not believing me, the more motivated I became to believe in myself—not to waste time proving them wrong. It was the same with friends or extended family. The more someone doubted, the more my faith increased. I had a life of unexplained spiritual experiences that felt realer than real to me. This was merely people's opinions and judgements that I had allowed myself to be overly concerned with. In truth, what little significance their opinions held to me. I began to look at work through an entirely new, more healthy light.

I felt graced to have had had spiritual experiences; they had given meaning to my life. And these memories could still instill a sense of grace and strength in the midst the ordinary challenges of life. Anytime I released my anger or frustration, I would take the time to replace the space with these positive memories.

PART X

Be transformed by the renewing of your mind.

Romans 12:2

We are disturbed not by what happens to us,
but by our thoughts about what happens.

Epictetus

The important thing is this: to be able, at any moment,
to sacrifice what we are for what we will become.

Charles Du Bos

FORGIVENESS IS A MAJOR THEME in Nadia Bolz-Weber's books. She also writes a lot about the dangers of being judgemental and how this mindset can keep us from reaching forgiveness.

It came down to understanding.

What was the reason behind people's behaviours? What was their perception of the world that they were operating under? Were they not wounded? As Bolz-Weber and a few other notable religious specialists reminded me, aren't we all simultaneously sinners and saints?

Bolz-Weber's words were instrumental to me towards challenging and changing my beliefs about forgiveness, and, more explicitly, how I viewed my relationship with my father. I had allowed my father's story to become my story. I had to change my thinking.

I was responsible for my own suffering; I had a right to feel fine. In reality, there was absolutely no reason to hold on to those thoughts I held about my father; they brought no peace into my life, only fear and unhappiness. I came to realize that it was my interpretations of the facts that were causing me stress.

Though I didn't know it at the time, I was doing "the work" that Byron Katie writes about in *Loving What Is*:

I had become too attached to my beliefs, for years.

Being mentally in my father's business had kept me from being in my own.

No thinking in the world was ever going to change reality. I had to accept that.

Everything outside of me had become a reflection of my thinking.

It was not about blame or guilt; it was all about acceptance, forgiveness, and peace.

My uninvestigated thinking, not my father's behaviour, was depressing me.

There was absolutely no positive reason to hang onto these beliefs about my father…these beliefs brought me zero peace.

As long as I thought that anyone or anything outside of myself was responsible for my suffering, the situation was hopeless.

I wasn't condoning my father's behaviour; he wasn't the issue. My happiness and personal growth were the issue. I had stopped loving myself the way I wanted others to love me.

If I could accept that this was my life, I would eventually be able to love my life as it was.

The school board and I finally reached an agreement as far as accommodations. I began a new job at the department of education by getting up every morning religiously at the same time as if I was driving to my office. I would shave, shower, and then dress for work, just in case I was called upon. It was like I was doing a very bad impression of my old working self. I was no longer a director, but I was still wearing his clothes. I was forced to accept that a part of me had remained attached to this image. Rarely did I ever receive a call or email that requested or required immediate assistance, at least not my direct presence. It's strange to look back, but though I didn't realize it at the time, I was living in the past, holding on to my former self, my role, my identity. People were busy; they had their own responsibilities and agendas. They knew where they could find me. It was my perceptions that had to change.

American hedge fund manager and best-selling author James Altucher has written many articles and blogs about the importance of reinventing yourself when starting over. He has written some very good advice. For starters, he said, when asked, never describe your present self by identifying with your past. Instead, choose who you are now.

"Every label you claim you have from before is just vanity."

Then he bluntly implies, besides, nobody really cares; people are more interested in who you are today. Don't try to be anything else.

It was important for me to look at myself through the eyes of my grandchildren. They were not remotely interested in who I had been; they were only interested in who I was now. Titles and status had absolutely no bearing on them. They only wanted someone who could be present and could love them unconditionally. This was who I truly was, this was what I valued, and this was how I wanted to perceive the world.

Showing up, being present—this was real.

There was a great sense of serenity about the hospice. My friend Mark's sister, Anne, was dying from cancer; she was now residing here. It was the same atmosphere as when my father stayed at the older centre: caring people continued to staff the place.

One afternoon, I went in to visit Anne, but she had company. I stood watching the pair from just outside the doorway. The scene reminded me of my mother and her special friend Bernice. Only this time it was Anne resting in the bed, and the special friend was Dorothy. Dorothy sat on the side of the bed feeding her ailing friend her lunch. I didn't dare disturb them. There was such ease in their togetherness.

The presence of a true friend can bring forth calming peace. It's good medicine.

In Albert Einstein's final years, he acknowledged in *Self-Portrait* that he lived "in the solitude which is painful in youth, but delicious in the years of maturity." It was important for me to realize the significance of solitude and accept how it differs from isolation.

I had always known that I required a considerable degree of solitude and quiet—not for thinking, but for listening. My strongest insights always happened naturally when I was quiet, open, and listening.

For this intense process of finding forgiveness for my father, I knew I would require an even greater degree or standard of peacefulness. I made a deliberate effort to restrict technology, avoided checking emails in the evening, and limited my distractions. I made an attempt to meditate daily, as brief as these sessions might have been, and to continue to exercise daily as well. Above all, I knew that I needed to be patient.

It was soon after that I first came across Henri J. M. Nouwen's *The Return of the Prodigal Son*. I was especially moved by his perspective on forgiveness. According to Nouwen, it was a chance encounter with a reproduction of Rembrandt's painting *The Return of the Prodigal Son* that had unexpectedly thrust him into a spiritual adventure. Nouwen came to believe that "the challenge in life is to love as the father and be loved as the son." In the conclusion, the author writes, "Do I want to be not just the one who is forgiven, but also the one who forgives; not just the one who is being welcomed home, but also the one who welcomes home?" Later he defines the responsibility of a spiritually adult person as one who trusts that "real joy and real fulfilment can only come from welcoming home those who have been hurt and wounded on their life's journey, and loving them with a love that neither asks nor expects anything in return."

The Prodigal Son is considered by many scholars to be the hardest of the Bible's parables, because forgiveness can be such a difficult concept to comprehend. For years, I behaved like the older son, in that I stood back and judged. I viewed my father's situation solely in terms of law, justice, and accountability rather than through the eyes of love, gratitude, and forgiveness.

Then one night in my solitude, while reading in bed, the final wall broke down. It was now clear to me. Yes, the issue had been forgiveness all along; however, in turn, I wanted to ask for my father's forgiveness as well.

That was yet another spiritual truth: I needed to forgive myself.

I wanted Father's forgiveness for how I continued to judge him and how I had neglected how wonderful he had made my early life and all he had done for me. It was time to stop judging the man and to stop judging the darker parts of myself as well. It had been years since I had truly acknowledged or accepted my father. I finally was able to look at him with empathy. He was a victim of depression and mental illness. I could clearly see that now. I took some of that personally when it wasn't personal at all. I acknowledged everything that he had to give up. The life he eventually lived was not the one he would have envisioned. If it had been enough, then why wasn't he happy? What a troubled soul he was.

Choosing not to live in a state of anger, hurt, and shame did not minimize the harm my father caused others, nor did it condone his actions. In choosing to heal and ask for forgiveness, my anger and shame had been replaced; I was consumed with nothing but a sense of love and gratitude. It was time to let go and to love him.

All people are flawed, but we are more than our brokenness.

The German philosopher Hegel put forth the argument that "war is evil," but upon deeper reflection, people generally come to realize that sometimes war is necessary and that good can and has come of war. The belief then becomes "war is good." The mind is forced to accept both contradictory facts. Hegel believed that the highest form of thought was when the values of both are brought together: "Despite the evils that come from war, there are certain values which men realize in war."

I had finally come to a stage in my own thinking where I could apply Hegel's example of war to religion: despite the many evils that had come from organized religion, there were clearly worthy values which people can and do realize in religion. Then I went even farther and began to apply this reasoning to the life of my father. I was not denying or condoning the actions of my father; I desired only to transcend the thought system that created my pain. I told myself that despite the wrongs that had come from my father's actions, there were many, many values and worthy qualities about my father. I put pen to paper and wrote down a series of random memories, only now I took the time to feel this new awareness in my body, to experience new meaning to these memories. I was changing my belief systems. I was no longer willing to be a prisoner of my past. I was willing to see things differently. When I allowed myself to assimilate and transcend both the thesis and the antithesis I had created about my father, I became calmer and more peaceful than I had been in years.

Often, my sleep was difficult. I was still experiencing "brain synapses," where my brain was firing off messages when it should have been at rest. It was not uncommon for me to be jolted awake from a deep sleep only to be left awake for hours. Other times, it would be dreams or messages that I would receive, and I might lie awake for a while trying to bring meaning to them.

This particular night it was something completely different that I experienced—what author Sonia Choquette might call "a powerful intuitive hit." All of my previous "communications" had proven to be factual or had at the very least provided a meaningful lesson. It made no sense to minimize the following experience. I just had no idea what to do with the information. This experience really jolted me.

My maternal aunt's husband committed suicide towards the end of the 1990s. He and my aunt were very close with my family, especially my mother. We were all shocked by his death, and the sudden loss naturally had a severe impact on his immediate family members.

Other than my parents, I had never had vivid communication dreams about the departed. This night, I had a powerful communication about my uncle. I cannot say that I communicated with him (my voices never identify themselves). It was, however, like I was receiving an understanding of him. It is so difficult to give verbal meaning to these experiences.

The communication began with the knowledge that my uncle was now doing well. That he was happy. But the strongest message I received was that *he didn't have to die*. It was his anger. While living, he had been consumed with unresolved anger. My uncle wanted me to know that he had accepted this. He also wanted me to know that he was still present with his children. That he had been to his daughter's recent graduation. And that he was concerned with one son's unresolved anger. The communication ended with the message that he wanted people, especially his loved ones, to learn from his mistakes.

The following morning I shared my experience with Cheryl. She knew that I was quite uncertain as to how to proceed. She was so supportive. She let it rest for a few days before asking me if I was going to share my experience with anyone else. She encouraged me to do so.

This was a major test for me. Who was I, to be believed by others in this regard?

"I honestly think it would be a good idea to share," Cheryl said.

Getting beyond my ingrained fears of rejection, I took the initiative and called my aunt. I shared with her what I had shared with Cheryl. My aunt was very open and welcomed what I had to share.

"You took quite a risk calling me."

"To be honest, I didn't know what to do."

"Thank you for doing that. I'm not sure how my children would react."

"I have been thinking about that. I thought that I would send an email to the two children who were mentioned in my communication and leave it up to them to contact me. First and foremost, I wanted to respect their comfort. I have no intentions of wanting to upset them—ever."

Both siblings responded to my texts. One reached out to me; the other one respectfully declined. I quite understood the rejection;

this wasn't about me. The sibling who was open arranged a time to call me later. I said what I had to say.

"I really felt Dad's presence at my graduation. Thank you for sharing."

This was a new level in unexplainable communication. Perhaps I was tapping into a greater level of evolved consciousness that is available to all of us. Perhaps it was a source of energy communicating with me. Regardless of the answer, my faith was being challenged. Unlike many of my previous "communications," there was no proof to convince me of the spiritual reality, no external support to my claim. It was a new level of acceptance.

The link between spirituality and happiness was the next spiritual truth that unfolded before me. The two were so interconnected. When I was calm and centred, living in the moment, I was happy. When I was trusting, kind, and compassionate to others, non-judgemental and open, honest with others and myself, I was happy. When I was with my animals and in nature, I was happy. When I surrounded myself with loving, caring people, I was happy. When I chose to be happy and took actions to affirm this, generally I was.

And when I was happy, I lived with meaning and purpose, I strived to be the best person I could be. My sense of spirituality came alive. I was alive.

Tuesday, October 14, 2014
St. Catherines

Today was going to be Cheryl and my first day in England as we celebrated our tenth anniversary, but because of my recent health flair-up, we had to cancel our trip. Instead I spent a wonderful day in another part of the world, our beautiful island. I met Cheryl and our two grandsons at the park before lunch. Then I took the dogs for a walk and spent some time moving and transplanting trees. Lots and lots of fresh air.

The old me would have taken ages to get over the disappointment of the cancelled trip.

Thursday, October 16, 2014
St. Catherines

Began the day with a beautiful one-hour walk with Nelly at Strathgartney Provincial Park. It was heavenly listening to the rain falling on the canopy of trees overhead. And watching Nelly running through the leaves.

I had a major realization today. Lately, I have been so discouraged with my lack of energy and inability to exercise. I have lost all of the strength and endurance that I gained last spring and summer. Today, I have accepted how sick I might be today had I not been exercising all along. I have to reframe my thinking. Instead of resenting my lack of energy, I need to look at how good my life is. Irony: if my health was better, I would have enjoyed returning to work, but would have worked long hours at a stressful job, which would not have been as good in the long run. I am where I need to be.

I also recognize how fortunate that I am to have Cheryl in my life. She has all the loving traits of my mother but is also supportive of my spiritual interests. She embraces my non-conformist side, something my mother struggled with.

It came back to living my own life journey and allowing others to take full responsibility for their own journeys; being in my business, not in others'. Life was not about control, definitely not about controlling others. It was learning from my life lessons, questioning for truth, trusting the answers. It was all coming together. Life is so interconnected.

Naturally, every experience we have changes us; our thoughts change us. And we are affected by every previous thought and experience we have ever had. Yes, our past influences our present selves, but now I was seeing that our present thoughts and experiences were also influencing our past—how we interpreted the past and how we allowed the past to affect the present day.

We can change our beliefs.

And when we change our beliefs, we change how the past affects us in the present.

The purpose of life is to continually redefine ourselves, to strive to become the grandest version of our self, to become everything we are capable of being. People do change.

It was more than experiencing divinity; it was more than intention; there was a responsibility to express our divinity as well.

There is so much truth in Marianne Williamson's statement that "the spiritual journey is a gentle reinterpretation of the world."

Towards the end of 2014 and into the beginning of 2015, I chose an act to really test my belief: I visited a naturopathic consultant who also happened to be a medium. A good friend of mine had recommended her. When I called beforehand, I shared that I had energy issues and was seeing medical specialists off-Island. I explained that I worked for the department of education and could use vacation time to see her. Other than that, I told the administrative assistant nothing else about myself. My first appointment was in November. I was completely out of my element, but intrigued just the same.

The naturopath began with a series of oil rubs on my forearms. The first insight that she shared, almost instantly, was that I had an allergy to mould, which had been medically proven. Then she surprised me by telling me that it came from my mother's side.

Then she clarified, "You were predisposed to mould, but it was your work environment that caused the illness." That made perfect sense.

Following a series of oil tests, the naturopath confirmed that I was also sensitive to caffeine, sugar, and chocolate. "Anxiety and stress are a concern for your condition. Your mother was a worrier. I would recommend meditation at least three times a week until it becomes a daily practice."

Afterwards, she did a reading upon my request.

"Your mother is with you twenty-four seven," she said. "She also helps your brother, but your father is looking over him."

That was the second hit: somehow she knew that my only sibling was male, though I had never told her.

Then she questioned, "Did you ever know your grandfather Smith?"

"No," I replied.

"He's interested in you as well."

That comment intrigued me. My father's father had died a few years before I was born. The only thing that I knew we shared was a strong intuitive nature and appreciation of the supernatural. As a young child, I remembered asking my father if my grandfather believed in the supernatural. And he answered, "More than any of us." But as I aged, my father's talk about his emotionally absent father had clouded my perception. I believe that I likely missed out on a lot not knowing him.

Then the conversation turned back to my health.

"Two years ago was extremely stressful for you."

This was another hit. I proceeded to share about being off work, the diagnosis I had received, the fight to retain my job, and losing consciousness while driving.

"But your health issues go much farther back. You were really sick twelve years ago, and the month of June was really stressful." This was information she couldn't possibly have known.

"That's when I first became ill, in 2002. I went off work in June."

I could not fathom how she knew these things. I was definitely in awe.

"As a child, you had severe anxiety at the age of five, starting in September."

"I started school when I was five." My rational mind told me that she could say this of any child and likely not be too far off.

"This was traumatic for you. Something to do with your relationship with your mom."

"We were completely co-dependent. I believed back then that she needed me at home."

"You have had two periods of severe grief: after your father's death and another beginning the day before your mother died."

I shared about my father's death, discovering his secrets afterwards, and then concealing them until my mother died.

"Would you mind if I did a card reading?"

"I would love that." And I sincerely meant it.

She shuffled the deck and began to place cards face up in front of me.

"The cards tell me that you have a love of knowledge and learning." I nodded. "You are being encouraged to devote time to a new career. Does this mean anything to you?"

"I will be retiring in less than two years, but I don't have any concrete plans for a new career. Just lots of ideas."

"The cards are indicating a new career; something in which you have a strong interest. Whatever you are interested in, they say to take courses or to continue reading on the subject matter.

"Your mother says not to worry about money. That there will always be enough to look after you and your family.

"As for your health, continue with what you are doing. Those magnesium treatments are excellent for you. There is no need for further medication."

I thanked the naturopath for our session. I had truly enjoyed myself and was amazed by her insights. I grabbed my coat and was heading to the door when she spoke again.

"There's one thing that does not make sense."

She paused to look at her referral pad.

"I generally won't share this, but I have never had such a definite reading. You told my secretary that you worked at the department of education. The message that I am receiving is that your purpose in life is to be in counselling, psychotherapy, or emotional healing."

"I have been a counsellor for most of my career. I only left the practice when I became ill."

"You have great capacity to love and to make a difference in this world."

Those were the warmest words I had ever heard.

My follow-up appointment was early in the New Year. The naturopath remarked how my overall energy seemed to be improving.

"Are you able to exercise?" she asked. "And do you do it regularly?"

"My energy level continues to improve, and, yes, I do continue to exercise."

She began once again to do a series of oil rubs, and every time was pleased with the overall improvement. "You are really doing well. Please continue with the healthy lifestyle. The only thing

I will suggest is that you truly begin to meditate at least three times a week."

"I will try again. Meditation is the one thing that I struggle to remain consistent with. I find it helpful, but I get restless, and repeatedly fail to commit long term."

"Just try." She smiled.

"Would you do a reading before I go?"

This time felt like more of a review—nothing too startling. Then she took the cards out again.

"Your mother has been trying to communicate with you. She tells me that she has been leaving a particular item around the house. She has been doing this to get your attention. Can you think of what it might be?"

Christmas had been busy. There were lots of people around, and lots of distractions. I closed my eyes and thought hard for a minute. Yes, there was one thing… dimes. I had been finding dimes all over the house, so much so that one morning I brought the matter to Cheryl's attention. Without sharing what it was, I answered, "Yes, there has been one item that comes to mind."

"Dimes," she said. "Your mom has been leaving dimes for you."

I knew that dimes could never be proof of an afterlife, but it was funny; allowing myself to embrace these signs provided me with a sense of peace and helped me to heal and move forward. I made a conscious effort to notice dimes in my future, and, more importantly, to allow myself to recognize how their presence made me feel. They became reminders of the beautiful mysteries of life.

I have since learned that dimes have a history in the paranormal; however, I had no idea at the time.

Carlye brought it to my attention that I was being too short with Cheryl. I took my daughter's criticism to heart and did a lot of self-reflection. I apologized to Cheryl for my recent behaviour, and we had a very open conversation. My illness could definitely affect my moods, but it was more than that. Cheryl and I were not communicating deeply with each other; we were both growing frustrated.

That night I picked up the book I had been reading: *A Return to Love* by Marianne Williamson. The next section was on "Holy Relationships." It was exactly what I needed to read.

I took the book to bed with me and read excerpts aloud to Cheryl. She equally loved and absorbed the messages—the importance of being "emotionally naked," that healing is the purpose of our being with another, to seek intimacy through acceptance and release, not control and guilt, and that we aim to help each other "access the highest parts within." We had to commit to work through any unhealed parts and not try to escape by denying or going around them.

September 30, 2015
St. Catherines

In my dream, I was travelling with a friend. In our travels, we came in contact with a couple, close to my own age. They were quite engaging, especially him. She was calm and centred and emitted a wonderful energy.

I noticed that she had set up an impromptu station to allow her to write. She told me that she was an author. She was travelling as was I, but she was committed to her passion to write.

"Writing gives me purpose and meaning," she said. "I still get to see new places. Enjoy the company of my lover. Enjoy the excitements associated with travel. I take my purpose

and meaning with me."

*I had given much of my time to travel as well, enjoy-
ing the pleasures of the new, but I was consumed with rest,
entertainment, and leisure activities. She was far more centred
and content than I.*

Thanksgiving weekend was exceptionally special. I turned fifty-
four on Monday, and in addition to a lovely dinner the night before,
we held a welcoming ceremony for the newest grandchild, Carlye
and Jon's Lennon, in their wedding grotto. Carlye kept the crowd
small. She invited the people who had been an influence in her life
and more importantly who she would like to have an influence in
Lennon's life. Her friends Steven and Birgit were in attendance; it
was Steven's first visit since acknowledging he was transgender. It
was a lovely celebration, and people stayed around afterwards for
snacks and drinks. Some stayed well into the evening, so we ordered
pizza. Then to top it all off, my godson called from BC to wish me
happy birthday and tell me that he and his wife were already expecting. "You're going to be a great-godfather!" The tears just
appeared.

In all this joy and happiness, there was still time to learn one
of my greatest lessons on love. And this involved a conversation
my brother-in-law had with Birgit, which he later shared with me.
Birgit had fallen in love with Rachel, who was now Steven, but she
had stayed with him; Karl was intrigued.

"How are you coping?" Karl asked.

"I'm wonderful," Birgit answered in her beautiful Swedish accent.

"Is life good living with Steven?"

She knew what he meant.

"I fell in love with the person, the spirit of the person, not the
gender."

In the beginning of 2016, the strongest of coincidences began to occur.

I was feeling more settled, definitely less stressed and anxious while being on sick leave. I was meditating one morning, and a close friend's father came to mind. I had only met him a handful of times, but this felt like an especially strong intuitive hit. I acknowledged the thought and returned to my meditation. The next morning I received a text from my brother informing me that this gentleman had passed away. While I had no direct relationship with this man, I was very close to his daughter and knew how extremely upset she would be. I immediately thought of my grandfather James Smith, and how he could predict the dead by times and how the naturopath/medium had told me he was coming through at my first reading.

Finding Forgiveness was in the hands of my editor, so that night I began preparing for a follow-up book. I had narrowed my focus but still wasn't pleased with any titles. From seemingly nowhere, I came up with the title *Spiritual Truths*. I liked the title but was still questioning my decision. In bed, I grabbed the book on my neighbouring nightstand, *Return of the Prodigal Son*, and opened it to where I had left off. I was tired, so I decided to only read a few pages. In the last paragraph I read the words, "spiritual truth."

I began to wonder how far synchronicities have to reach before people truly take notice.

It was Monday, January 25. I had recently been getting some dental work done, and, by accident, I called my dentist's cell phone instead of his office; I reached him as he was waiting for a flight at the Houston International Airport. He laughed at my mistake, and then said, "I don't know why I didn't think of you."

"Think of me why?"

"I'm down here for specialized training; then my instructor is coming to the Island to do training with my staff. He has asked me to find a few volunteer patients. He would like to have someone who suffers from brain fog. You told me that you suffered from brain fog, but I totally forgot. Would you be interested?"

"Very much," I assured him.

My misplaced phone call provided me with the opportunity to meet with a specialist interested in brain fog. I had to be available for three-and-a-half hours on a Friday afternoon. The only other thing asked of me was to give up eating gluten for the two weeks prior to my appointment, which I agreed to.

The eventual session with the specialist ended up being both mind-boggling and life changing. While looking at X-rays of my mouth, he declared, "We have a major problem here." Sitting in a nearby dental chair, I overheard him and assumed his comment had to do with my teeth.

But he continued.

"This man has been exposed to major chemicals."

Simply by looking at X-rays of my mouth, this specialist was able to flawlessly diagnosis my condition and identify my past health patterns as well as aspects of my parents' health history. I couldn't believe what I was hearing.

He began by telling me that my mouth and nose were quite inflamed. He told me this likely indicated that my brain was as well. This would explain the headaches, brain fog, and broken sleep patterns.

I sat there somewhat spellbound as he described what he felt was the state of my work conditions, conjecturing that it was likely asbestos and mould that I was exposed to, that I likely returned to work to a modern building where there was water damage, that my office building probably had water pipes overhead that had burst or leaked, and the tiles were those large, white, square tiles that were easily replaced to cover the water stains. He was 100 per cent accurate.

"Of course," he added, "no one wanted to take responsibility."

Then he asked about family history and the diet of my parents. When I shared their meat-and-potatoes diet with lots of white bread and flour and sugar, he simply asked, "And how well did that serve them?"

"They were both dead from cancer before the age of sixty."

"You'll risk a similar circumstance if you don't change your diet today."

I felt like I had been hit with a sledgehammer.

"And I mean a radical change."

He explained that nothing happened in isolation. You have to consider a person's genetic heritage, their home and work environments, and their lifestyle choices: diet, exercise, stress management, alcohol and drug consumption, etc. He explained that my Gaelic roots may have made me more susceptible to mould and asbestos as well as increasing my sensitivity to gluten. My genetics made me more susceptible, and the work exposure to chemicals had now made me completely vulnerable, likely more vulnerable than about 95 per cent of the general population.

The doctor asked about Fall River. I shared my experiences, and he was quite impressed. He advised me to continue with everything they recommended, especially the exercise, but to be even more restrictive with my diet. Since the causes and advancement of many illnesses are multifactorial, it only stood to reason that the secret to healing would be as well.

"Gluten is the real issue," he said. "When you first came off gluten, you felt amazing, right? But it didn't last."

I agreed. I shared that nearing the end of the second week, I honestly thought I had been cured, but then it came back. I was so discouraged I cried on the stairs leading to my bedroom.

The specialist explained, "After a while, your body starts to process sugar in the same manner. You need to continue to exercise and remove gluten and all sugar, not just refined sugar, from your diet. You need to stop those jolting-awake brain synapses. They're very damaging."

I sat there quietly nodding my head, trying to absorb everything that he was saying.

"You need to clean up your gut. The gut is like your second brain. I'm going to recommend daily supplements for at least three months to help clean out your bowels."

This specialist may have added years to my life, but the immediate difference was the return to a quality to my life that I hadn't known in years. I would be forever grateful to this man and to my dentist. What were the odds of this meeting taking place?

Being told that I could be dead before sixty was also quite motivating on another level. This was an area that I felt my present family could not totally relate to. Both of my parents had died of cancer before the age of sixty. I was fifty-four.

Often when people overcome an illness, there is a desire to make the most of time—either to reclaim lost time or an increased awareness of the futility of life. Either way, there is a desire to make a difference. It made me realize that there were lots of things that I wanted to do before my life was over. I was filled with a tremendous appreciation for life. The heightened awareness of my own mortality had strengthened my innate sense of purpose, launching me into my own deeper spiritual search for meaning. This became my passion as it reflected what, other than my family, was most important in my life.

Part XI

There is a healing field for each of the three wounds.
Commitment heals abandonment, honour heals shame,
and loyalty heals betrayal.

Dr. Mario Martinez

When we deny our stories, they define us.
When we own our stories, we get to write a brave new ending.

Brené Brown

IT WASN'T A MATTER OF SHAME, cowardice, or even fainthearted-
ness. It was a simple matter of respect. When I made the decision
to publish a book on my relationship with my father, there were
only three people who might have stopped me: Cheryl, Hayden,
and my uncle, Father Brady Smith. Hayden and Father Brady
because this book detailed a big part of their lives, too, and I would
never want to hurt them.

The Catholic Church was everything to Father Brady. He
believed that it and AA had saved his life. Together, they had given
him a tremendous sense of purpose and meaning, an opportunity
to help others. He exemplified the wounded healer that Henri J.
M. Nouwen writes about.

Father Brady passed away in the early morning of Sunday, March
16, 2016. It was the same week my final revision with a private
freelance editor came back. A part of me had been holding off.
Now there was nothing to hold me back.

In the spring of 2016, my spirituality was tested—and I really mean that my ego was testing me.

I had been off work since mid-December. My health was definitely improving, but one of the primary factors for this change was that I was off work. I was removed from a significant degree of stress in my life and now had the flexibility to rest and exercise when my body needed it. I could listen to my body. At the time, I had twenty-nine-and-a-half years of service in education, and my career was ending on an extremely low note. It felt like a kind of death, and a death without closure. I was grieving; however, grief is an opportunity to transform you, to learn who you really are, what you value, and how you will come to perceive the world.

Julia and I had worked together for years. When I went off on sick leave, she replaced me as director. And now she was in my living room, inquiring about my health, questioning if I was ready to return to work, offering me a wonderful work opportunity to finish out my career. Even the deputy minister of the day had remarked that this position was made for me. I would be representing education and working with other agencies to collaborate on services for students deemed to be at risk. This was a mandate I had been lobbying for for most of my professional career—a good portion of my life. I could even work part-time, and they would guarantee a healthy air environment. There was one catch: I would have to delay my retirement and commit to this project for at least an additional year to assure that the project was up and running.

To be considered for this role was an honour. It was an opportunity to finish my career on a positive note, to—I would hope—earn back some people's support and respect, rectify my self-perceived fall from grace. I thought seriously about the offer. I spoke with Cheryl, and I even ran the idea by a few close family members and friends.

But it was all ego doing the talking. It was all about my reputation, my image, the role, and the title. How much of all that was I truly willing to let go?

I had spent enough time with medical specialists and read enough literature to know how stress and the fight-or-flight response had impacted and would continue to impact my immune system. The longer I stayed in protection mode, the more energy my body was consuming, which would compromise my growth in other areas.

After a few days of serious reflection, I was convinced more than ever that returning to my old line of work, even if it was significantly modified, was not the correct route for me; it was not the answer. This was not a time of death; this was an opportunity for rebirth.

The greatest awareness for me was that although the past four years had been challenging in terms of health, in hindsight, I would not change anything if I had to go back to being who I was before I took sick.

That was the depth of my transformation.

It took a lot to admit that.

Dennis was medically discharged from the military in 2013, and, since that time, he has worked hard, very hard, to demilitarize himself. He returned home knowing that in war, scars are inevitable: physically, emotionally, mentally, and/or spiritually. Like many of his comrades, Dennis was diagnosed with PTSD as a result of the experiences he endured; however, Dennis's condition actually was elevated by how he was treated back on Canadian soil. Feelings of shame, anger, and anxiousness were heightened because of the stigma associated with the diagnosis. Within the army culture, he and others were not encouraged to ask for help or to draw attention to their emotional struggles. That was an indication of weakness. Rather than being encouraged to grieve together and to support one another, he felt shunned; it basically meant the end of his military career.

Known for his caring and empathetic disposition, upon returning to civilian life, Dennis considered employment in the field of counselling, but the severity of his PTSD struggles, and now being a single parent to two young boys, were major life hurdles. Then in the summer of 2015, Dennis was contacted by a close friend and former military colleague, and, after an hour-and-a-half conversation, Dennis was convinced to try medical marijuana, as it had done wonders for his friend's PTSD symptoms. Dennis was not a cannabis user. He was actually against the use of marijuana, but he was also completely ignorant of its medicinal potential. He was extremely fortunate to have a clinical psychologist who was very, very supportive of cannabis for veterans living with PTSD. She came into his life when he needed her. She had seen first-hand the wonders that medical marijuana had done for other clients and actively promoted a holistic, natural approach to treatment.

Life turned around for Dennis in January 2016, when a friend who was involved in Marijuana for Trauma (MFT) in St. Catharines, Ontario, suggested that Dennis contact a lad by the name of Fabian about establishing a clinic on PEI. By the end of the month, Dennis had sent out 192 self-addressed letters to Island doctors seeking to determine their level of interest and support for medical marijuana. Not one reply. But he was determined. He was committed. He endured.

It was the beginning of an immense spiritual journey for Dennis, and it was beautiful to watch it unfold. Dennis began to transcend many of his own personal demons by reaching out to other veterans experiencing similar struggles. It was yet more proof that regardless of what degree of turmoil and anguish we may find ourselves in, we can still find a sense of meaning and purpose in our lives if we are willing to take the risk.

The next month, our family returned to the Riu Merengue resort beach in the Dominican Republic for a family reunion. Riley and Nikki flew from BC and the rest of us left from Halifax. It was Grampy's treat for the three male grandchildren. This, however, was a source of stress for Dennis. For the first time in years he had found some relief from his PTSD symptoms, but he couldn't travel with cannabis, and while marijuana may be a common street drug in Dominican Republic, possession of any amount is illegal.

It was a few days into our trip, and a group of us had gathered on the deck of Dennis's room. He didn't look great. He wasn't sleeping; he feared he was losing all the gains he had recently made.

I knew his anguish was real, so I excused myself. I had been travelling to the Caribbean once a year for the past ten years or more, and, in all those years, I had never seen cannabis on these private resorts. I followed my intuition and went into the main lobby. Within fifteen minutes, a Dominican man who was now living in Canada and just home on vacation approached me. He asked if I wanted to buy marijuana. I knew that it was breaking the law, but I knew my son needed it for his well-being. This wasn't just chance; this man came into my path for a reason. I asked him where my son could meet him. It was meant to happen.

MFT's main office was located in Oromocto, NB, not far from the Gagetown Army Base that Dennis had been stationed at when he was enlisted. Dennis had been invited over for some training, and Cheryl and I had gone along to help look after the boys. It was June 15, 2016, and Dennis and I were attending a MFT social night. We were staying in a hotel in nearby Fredericton. I was wide awake after the stimulation of all the newness and decided to go for a late evening run. It was close to ten when I left the hotel, but the boardwalk that lined the river was well lit. Besides, I had run along here many times when I had studied at the local university.

I ran twenty minutes in one direction and then retraced my path. On my return, I came to a darkened section of the boardwalk and literally froze; my mind or body would not permit me to move forward. I stopped dead in my tracks and just stood there. For no logical explanation, I had the most obscure sensation that a car might lose control on the sharp turn just above the walkway, that it might soar over the embankment and hit me. It was like I was experiencing an anxiety attack.

Get a grip, I told myself. I reminded myself that I run at night all the time, in all types of weather, in various locations. That scenario or something similar could happen anywhere. *Why lose it here?* I scolded myself.

I was really troubled. I eventually collected myself and headed back to the room where Cheryl, Dennis, and the boys were waiting. Declan was having a ball mimicking the NBA stars on television; it was easy to blend in and get wrapped up and distracted with my grandson. I elected to tell no one of my experience. And then proceeded to have a very restless sleep.

The next evening we were back to the hotel much earlier than the night before. My energy was still off; this time I decided to go for a walk along the same route I had run the night before. It was only eight o'clock, and the evening was bright and warm. As I approached the location on the boardwalk where I had stopped the previous night, I noticed a lot of broken branches lying about that I hadn't observed in the darkness of the previous night.

Then I noticed a gentleman taking pictures down by the water, so I ventured over towards him.

"What happened here?" I asked.

"Didn't you hear?"

"I'm not from here. I'm just visiting."

"A young girl was killed here last weekend."

The man veered around and pointed to the turn on the road—the very spot where I froze the night before.

"The driver lost control on that turn, the car flew through the air, breaking that light post." He then pointed to the top of the pole that had been clipped by the car travelling through the air, which explained the darkened section of the boardwalk. Then he turned towards the broken branches and the neighbouring water. "They flew through that tree into the water. The young passenger girl was thrown from the car."

That was the intense energy I had felt the night before.

I had had lots of experience picking up present or current energy; this was the first time I was aware of having sensed past or lingering energy. It was yet another example of the energy that exists and connects us in this world. It was yet another unexplained experience that proved to me that there was so much more to this world than we understand. Energy does not cease.

As I shared previously, Dr. Mario Martinez writes that there is a "healing field" for our three archetypal wounds: "abandonment, betrayal, and shame." In his opinion, the respective antidotes are commitment, loyalty, and honour. *Honour* heals shame. As I did some research on the term *honour*, though I didn't know where it was leading me, it all came together. That's where *Finding Forgiveness* came in.

When I say that I wrote *Finding Forgiveness* as a means to find honour, I am by no means using the term to imply seeking glory or fame or title; I was searching for the complete opposite (which

I am confident Martinez was referring to as well). I was writing my book as a means of finding a sense of personal worthiness and integrity, a means to dignify my soul. Writing my story was the most authentic act I could take.

I had struggled to find forgiveness for my father, but I found it; then, I worked hard to forgive myself. Now it was time to go even deeper, as deep as I could go. In truth, my earliest wound was shame. As a young child, I was completely open to others, but as a preteen and teenager, I allowed myself to be ashamed of my home—my father being so different and clandestine, the lack of physical affection among my parents, a home so sheltered and cloistered, the fact that no one truly got in, Mother always concerned with what the neighbours thought. That sense of shame carried through and intensified after I learned of my father's past—his lies and secrets, then the allegations against him. And I had chosen to live out the lie—putting up walls, trying to protect everyone.

Then I learned that the origin of the word *honour* derives from the Latin word, *magnanimous*, which means "generous in forgiving." However, there are some differing usages of the term, and some people have argued that the word *honour* needs to be seen more as rhetoric—the art of using words in speaking or writing—as opposed to a code of conduct. And that was, without question, my sincere intent. It felt like those words were written for me.

No significant meetings are accidental. We never know where our next inspiration may come from, or who might stimulate our desire for growth. The secret is to remain open and welcome these opportunities into our lives.

On Sunday, August 7, 2016, I was attending a fifth wedding anniversary for my first cousin and her husband when I had an encounter with her brother, Donn Smith, who is a counsellor with a strong spiritual core. It was pure synchronicity: first of all, I had attended the event alone. My initial plans involved attending with both Cheryl and my brother, but the day before Cheryl had come down with a bad summer cold, and Hayden had been called into work. I would never have had the same interaction with Donn if either of them had accompanied me. It simply would never have transpired.

This was one stage of my journey that I was meant to take alone.

Donn was aware of my health issues. I had made tremendous progress and was following my stringent diet and exercise regimes, yet my symptoms were still lingering. Donn believed that there was some enduring emotional residue and more work to be done. He offered to work with me if I was open to the challenge. So after the celebration, we drove out to Canoe Cove and overlooked the sun setting on the south shore. Donn was about to carry out a series of mind-body exercises, and he wanted to be close to water. I was completely out of my comfort zone, doing these therapeutic exercises in public. There were my first fears or limiting beliefs: the desire for conformity and fear of judgement.

Other than the public display, I was very comfortable with Donn's approach. His philosophy totally supported all of the medical advice I had received both from Fall River and the San Diego specialist, and his counselling methods were reflective of what had worked for me in the past. He believed in mind-body approaches, visualization, left-brain and right-brain engagement, and confronting or challenging the client to go deeper. Afterwards, there would be great emphasis on committing to meditation, reflective journal writing, forgiveness, and practicing letting go. The approach appealed to me, for I knew from personal and work experiences that knowledge had to be transferred into emotional or subconscious knowledge. Intellectual knowledge was not enough.

I knew I had to feel a bodily reaction to retain the knowledge. I referred to it as "feeling the feeling"—there are surface feelings and then there are bodily reactions at a subconscious level.

Then I remembered that eighteen years before, in Terrace, BC, a psychic had identified these very same issues: *It is too easy for you to resort to your mind or intelligence and to analyze your feelings… Your greatest block or threat is your own fear… You care too much about what society thinks… Pay closer attention to your body and emotional states… What are they telling you?*

What was different about Donn's approach and served to be key for me was the crucial emphasis on spirituality. He wanted me to begin to honour my own intrinsic value and to foster a more open relationship with God/Spirit. Not just think and talk about it. Donn challenged me to grow spiritually and to live the life I had been meaning to live. That was key.

Under Donn's mentoring, I meditated two or three times a day (always before bed and in the morning) for at least ten minutes at a time. I kept a pen and pad of paper beside me and wrote down any insights that I received. In addition, I also wrote a journal reflection every day and did a daily text exchange with Donn. The intent was to take ownership of my thoughts and experiences and to have a record of all the changes. The process of writing down my thoughts had always helped bring clarity. If I had a record of all the experiences, synchronous events, insights and intuitions, then any doubt would eventually be removed. I believed that, in the end, this journal would be a documented record for me that would eventually provide the proof I had reluctantly been searching for. I also wanted to have a complete sense of gratitude for what I was experiencing.

But it was more than that. It had been years, what felt like a lifetime, since someone had believed that much in my spiritual development. I can't say enough about the power of having someone you trust believe in you: what a powerful spiritual truth.

I would say that for the past number of years I had spiritually flat-lined; from a spiritual perspective, I was standing still, idling at best. I thought I knew what I wanted, but I truly didn't know how to get there. I may have had belief and faith, but I had no real meaningful relationship with my concept of God/Spirit. I didn't know how to get to the next level, and I certainly didn't want to wait for another crisis to jumpstart me. I truly desired to focus on all the good that I had. I came to believe that I had to truly honour my spiritual experiences if my life was ever going to feel fully fulfilled.

It soon became obvious that the commitment to meditation was key. Meditation became that overlap between the "exotically metaphysical and the naturalistic" that Robert Wright writes about. Meditation convinces the mind that the body is safe. It stops the fight-or-flight response that my central nervous system had been stuck on; simultaneously, it was strengthening my intuition. As Wright points out, meditation is more than focusing on your breath: "it's to stabilize your mind, to free it of its normal preoccupations so you can observe things that are happening in a clear, unhurried, less reactive way." It is a means for translucency and insight. It is the merging of two worlds.

When I fully opened myself up to Spirit, the change was immediate. Messages were continually being reinforced. Dreams were more meaningful; synchronicities abounded; intuition came stronger.

Though key, meditation alone was not the answer; it was meditation with the support of other spiritual practices. Without the daily morning reflections, it would not have been the same. Writing down my thoughts and taking another level of ownership for them was bringing clarity. I gained an awareness and appreciation of what I had been doing right all along: gratitude journal, daily exercise, diet, prayer, counselling from both sides of the desk, and detaching. I believed that if I continued to honour my rituals, I would break the psychic mould that allows familiar thinking and behavioural patterns to quickly return. I could override and replace that circuit.

In *There's More to Life than This*, medium Theresa Caputo eloquently writes that she believes God had given her a canvas, but that it was up to her to paint a beautiful picture. There was something missing in the landscape until *she* did the work that satisfied *her* soul.

We are all faced with painting our own canvases.

So I had to ask myself, *what would satisfy my soul?*

Few things satisfied my soul more than counselling. But I wasn't willing to do more of the same; I needed a deeper, more immediate and intense spiritual aspect to my work: spiritual counselling outside of any dogma or religious creed.

We are all energy. Even our thoughts and emotions are first and foremost energy. Counselling, like healing, implies identifying what energy is stuck, removing negative energy, and replacing it with good energy. We help keep our physical bodies healthy by keeping our spiritual energy flowing and free.

Our greatest spiritual healers are ourselves.

And then it hit me.

That experience at the bookstore in the summer of 1994, when the exceptional number of pertinent book titles—incest, suicide, bereavement, addictions, sexual abuse, and dysfunctional sexual relationships—had overwhelmed my brain, and just as suddenly all of the books before me seemed to mesh together, as if all those themes had the same underlying derivation, which had been previously been unknown to me, but was revealed that afternoon: that the true nature or purpose of counselling was to be viewed from this deeper, spiritual perspective and awareness.

The Return of the Prodigal Son would prove to have a tremendous impact on me. The subtitle of Nouwen's book is *A Story of Homecoming,* and at this stage of my spiritual journey, I truly was experiencing a homecoming of sorts.

It was Saturday, November 5, 2016. An older brother of a good friend had passed away in Ontario, and his funeral was being held in my childhood church, St. Augustine's. I could not remember the last time I had been inside of this church. Other than my childhood home and the northern shore of PEI, no other location brought forth stronger memories and associations of my father; however, on this day, I truly was looking forward to going back to my roots.

Driving out, I was thinking of others I have known who have gone through their own spiritual journeys that, at the time, I didn't understand or relate to. The one person who came readily to mind was Bernice, Mom's close friend who sat with her for hours as Mother prepared to die. I acknowledged to myself how much respect and admiration I had for her and for others who persevered and remained true to themselves.

I parked the car and walked into the church alongside a childhood friend. We sat down together towards the back of the church. Inside, the atmosphere was warm and inviting. I sat back in my seat, closed my eyes, and just breathed deeply for a while before saying a morning prayer. I became aware of how exceptionally calm and peaceful I felt. Having finished, I opened my eyes and had a look around. Who was sitting two pews in front of me but Bernice. I smiled to myself and then took another look around. What did I see but a reproduction of Rembrandt's painting, *The Return of the Prodigal Son*, hanging on the left pillar closest to the altar. The last time I had seen this image was on the cover of Nouwen's book.

I had come home.

Many great spiritual writers have written about how people long to come home, return to God, return to Love. I was intrigued to learn that writers like Scott Peck and Ken Wilber wrote about the need to *transcend but include* one's initial experience of home, a theory that can be applied to spirituality. For me, it was not simply a matter of returning to my childhood roots, my childhood church—it was a matter of coming home with everything I had learned, experienced, and transcended, and then assimilating all of this into my beliefs.

A gay friend of mine once sat on his parents' front steps and shared with me how he felt like he could never come home. The old me could not have come home either. That would have been impossible. But the new me, the authentic me, could come home and even feel welcome.

How I wanted to help my friend and others feel the same way.

The truth was that my spiritual life did not now exist as a return to church or the joining of any religious institution. It was not dependent on yoga or a meditation altar in the sanctuary of my home. It did not require extended moments of solitude or mindfulness retreats. While all of the mentioned are valuable in their own worth and offer inspiration, it was much deeper than that. For me, I needed to find forgiveness in my heart and then live out that truth. I had to show up. I had to be present to what was real.

In *Tears to Triumph*, Marianne Williamson writes, "Mercy is a word that means very little until we have actually felt it. And once we do, we are changed forever." That's what it was like with forgiveness. It is difficult to explain the experience. It's that "aha" moment. You just know it when it happens.

It is difficult to explain receiving a message advising me to intervene on behalf of my mother. It is difficult to explain having a sense of "knowing" and trusting enough to act out that knowing in every moment of your life. It is difficult to explain the sense of peace that you can attain when you truly let go of nagging doubts and believe. It is difficult to explain how living forgiveness beyond the saying of the words can change your life.

People change.

Transformation is difficult. You have to really want it. You have to commit.

I had changed.

My mother had changed on her deathbed. For the first time in her life, she allowed herself to truly question. It was the most honest she had ever allowed herself to be about her childhood home; she had moved beyond her fears and self-defeating beliefs. She had also been able to see and acknowledge what purpose my writing served for me.

However, the greatest personal teaching of this truth came through my oldest son, as he struggled to overcome his PTSD symptoms. Afghanistan had been hell. He now had to live with what he had witnessed and been involved with during that horrendous time. He was at my house one afternoon, and we were alone, sharing a deep, meaningful conversation.

In a peaceful, sincere tone, Dennis said to me, "I could not go on if I didn't believe that I could change... that the old version of myself, the soldier, had ceased to exist."

For the first time in his journey, Dennis was allowing himself to acknowledge his spiritual nature and permitting it to come through, to rise to the surface.

Dennis had changed; I had changed. I could finally believe that my father, too, had changed. Removed of my preconceived notions, my unexamined beliefs, my judgements, I was able to conceive a new version of my father, one that I believed had more clarity, one that I believed was closer to the truth.

In *Vaster Than Sky, Greater Than Space,* Jamaican spiritual teacher Mooji writes, "If an authentic search is emerging in you, it's ultimately going to come with a fight." The fight is the struggle to remain as you are and the pull of liberation. Later in his book, Mooji expands on this thinking, sharing that a "tremendous resistance will arise when you come to some defining moment in your life." He views these challenges "as mirrors to look at your own Self."

This was clearly a defining moment in my life.

As the date of my book release neared, my brother's anxieties had risen to the surface; he was a shadow of the man I had known, the person who had been a primary supporter every step along the way. Now he was a troubled man, consumed with fears of the possibility of negative public reaction, backlash, and rejection.

"You left," Hayden reminded me in a less than pleasant tone. "I still live in this community."

That was true. I had left. He was still living in our childhood surroundings.

I gave him a way out.

"Tell people that you have to work. If it causes you such stress to attend my book launch, then stay away. I mean it. Had I known the book would have caused this reaction, I wouldn't have gone through with it. All you ever had to say was stop, and I would have. You know that."

Della could understand the emotions her husband was enduring, but she could also empathize with what I was going through. Recognizing the position I was now in, she spoke up in my defence, gently reminding Hayden that I had included him in every step along the way. While I truly appreciated the support, it wasn't necessary, as my brother knew I was being sincere and telling the truth. He didn't have to attend.

Hayden's fears lingered for days. Even on the morning of the launch, I spoke with him, and he was still uncertain that he would be able to attend.

It was that same old pattern: at defining moments in my life, I was being tested. Evolve or repeat. In the past, that contrasting element that forced me to recheck my beliefs had been my aunts coming to my house sharing allegations of abuse against my father just prior to my e-book being released, or my friend and colleague from work offering me a work position that "was made for me" when I had committed to walking away. This time, it was my brother's anguish that tested my conviction.

On May 25, 2017, Acorn Press held a book launch for *Finding Forgiveness* at a quaint room upstairs in an Irish pub, the Old Triangle. There was a lovely turnout of family and friends; in truth, it was all I could have hoped for. The publisher was amazing to work with, and the media gave me great coverage. That evening, after everyone had gathered, drinks in hand, and was settling in, I intermediately scanned the pub looking for my brother; he hadn't come. I accepted his decision; I had to move on.

Then, just as my publisher was introducing me, Hayden and Della entered my vision. Apparently, they had been late arriving and had been mingling towards the rear of the room. I was ecstatic.

I spoke a few words at the launch: welcomed everyone, acknowledged my readers, editors, and publisher, and introduced my family. I also explained why I felt I needed to share my story—for I knew there were many who questioned and would question my need. Basically, there were three intersecting reasons:

- Personal growth. Living with secrets had negatively affected me emotionally, physically, mentally, socially, and spiritually.
- Creativity. Writing was therapeutic.
- Wanting to help others. I needed to make meaning out of my suffering.

I shared about how, when my mother was dying, I had come upon the book *On Grief* by C. S. Lewis and how he wrote that when you actually learn how someone else has suffered and yet survived, this can actually help as you begin to crawl up from your pain and suffering. And then years later in an Ottawa bookstore I discovered Colm Tóibín's *Love in a Dark Time* and could only then fully relate to what C. S. Lewis had written. Since that day of awareness, I wanted my story to help others like Tóibín's book had helped me. I wanted my book to serve as a guide. Sharing my pain was to be understood as a way to liberation. It was my personal means of eradicating my fears. Like Henri J. M. Nouwen and *The Wounded Healer*, I had longed for my story to be "the way to health, to liberation, and new life."

A close childhood friend shared that she personally needed to hear the reasons why I had written my book. "I was meant to hear that," she said, "and when people in the community question, I now have the answer."

In *Braving the Wilderness*, Brené Brown writes, "The transformative power of art is in the sharing… It's the sharing of art that whispers, 'You're not alone.'"

The next morning, a cousin of mine sent me a text sharing how impressed he was with the evening, and "the outpouring of love you have for your family and friends, and they have for you. I was glad to witness this."

A friend of one of my sons sent another text saying, "I have never been in a room with so much love."

The most meaningful quote of the night, however, came from Della. Speaking of her husband, she said, "The darkness has already lifted from his eyes."

It was true. My brother could not get over the emotional support that abided in that room. The following morning he called me. "If I had not asked for the four hours off work and had not attended, it would have been among the biggest disappointments in my life." Telling the truth was making a difference already; freedom was manifesting in my life.

Over the coming weeks, I generally received at least one personal reflection a day from a reader. Often they came from past acquaintances or childhood connections. Sometimes it would be from someone who was a stranger to me but who had known my father. Sometimes it was from someone with no connection to my family or me.

One of the most meaningful messages came from a close friend who knew both Father and myself. "It was a great read, Adrian, and interesting to see how all of this has impacted your life. I'm so happy that you were able to find forgiveness and now live a life sharing with all those who love you."

I reread the ending of her text again.

There was so much truth in her innocent and candid words. It was a lot to absorb. She was absolutely correct in her thinking. There was never any question of love; it was merely a matter of identifying and removing the barriers that I myself had created. I loved my friends, but I had not allowed myself to feel openly loved by them. That was going to change. I was now going to live my life on an entirely new level, one I had never before been brave enough to enter before. I was going to let people completely in.

I had finally come home, but I did not want to return empty-handed. Poet, philosopher, and cancer survivor Mark Nepo believes that if we journey without being changed, we exist as a nomad. If we change without the journey, we are no more than a chameleon. Our innate desire is to journey and to be transformed by the experience… to be a pilgrim. There was now a strong desire to make a difference. I wanted to share all that I had learned. Now I wanted to help my friends, loved ones, even strangers who came into my life, to follow and to embrace their journeys and to find their truths. I especially didn't want young people to wait as long as I did if it was at all possible.

This was an opportunity for me to bring everything together in my version of spiritual counselling. My counselling approach would become a mosaic of many deeply connected tiles:

- Identifying the wound, confronting/removing the attachment, and replacing with self-worth
- Moving from a preoccupation with the past to feeling a sense of sincere hope for the future
- Knowing your "capacity to love has not been destroyed"
- Trusting intuition
- Investigating belief systems
- Using a mind-body approach

- Forgiving
- Finding self-actualization through self-transcendence

This was my calling. I couldn't live any other way and expect to know peace and happiness. This was who I am. I think if we are truly happy and content then that is how we desire our family, friends, and everyone who comes into our lives to be. We are all one.

Life in and of itself is a blessing.

In the prologue to this book, I shared how Maslow claimed that if our basic needs are met— namely, physiological, safety, love, and esteem—then humans will experience the need to become everything that one is capable of becoming: "What a man can be, he must be." Maslow referred to this need as self-actualization. It amazes me how his principles reflect the philosophy of the chakras.

Many forms of Hinduism and Buddhism believe in a life force, an energy that exists in all living things and keeps us alive. Chakras, or energy centres, allow this energy to travel through our bodies. According to ancient traditions, there are seven main chakras, and the flow and alignment of these seven chakras are critical to our health and vitality. Our energy can get blocked at any one of these levels because of unresolved issues associated with each particular centre.

In *Becoming Supernatural*, Dr. Joe Dispenza asks the pertinent question, "But what happens when we do more with our energy than just survive?" He then proceeds to explain how our energy can evolve from our initial survival centres upwards to our more divinity centres, a process available to all of us.

This is a brief summary of how my life and spiritual journey was unfolding according to this perspective:

Like everyone, my energy begins at my root chakra, and once I felt safe and secure enough I ascended into the second centre, which is related to our social relationships, family, cultures, and interpersonal relationships. It is the centre for "holding on or letting go" of our attachments. Once I felt more secure in my surrounding environment, I wanted to move on; however, as I aged, my third centre would have repeatedly wanted to protect myself for I had so many unresolved issues that clearly blocked my energy flow: my dysfunctional, enmeshed childhood; omissions of truth; teenage and young adult complications of alcohol abuse and promiscuity; young adult history of betrayal and secrets. With all of that emotional turmoil and disorder existing, there was no way that I could be the best version of myself; there was no way that I could heal.

It was only when I had successfully transcended the gift of adversities in my life, which Dispenza reminds his readers are experiences that challenge us to grow and overcome, did I have the opportunity to feel whole, free, and real. The fourth energy centre is the heart, perhaps the most important, for this is where our divinity originates, and we are moving "from being selfish to being selfless." Then, and only then, could I love unconditionally and return to that degree of love.

The fifth centre, which is located at our throat, wants us to express the love we felt in the fourth centre and voice our present truth through language. That is where *Sins of Omissions* and *Finding Forgiveness* came in. I needed to honour myself. For only then could I advance to the sixth chakra, where, unblocked, I could see the world with a broader perspective than I normally knew. At this stage our intuition and inner wisdom is strongest. The seventh energy centre represents our ability to be fully connected spiritually, and live in a sense of balance and harmony with ourselves, the people we choose to surround ourselves with, and nature. I had had repeated sightings of this stage but now I wanted to try to abide here forever.

Dispenza believes that once we experience that enlightened energy we actually activate an eighth centre, "Where we receive the fruits of our efforts—visions, dreams, insights, manifestations, and knowingness that come not from anywhere within our minds and bodies as memories but from a greater power in and around us." My reluctant search for spiritual truth was over. I acknowledged and accepted that this was what I had all along been searching for, and I was willing to continue to work hard to remain here as much as I could. We all have access to this universal spiritual energy if we are willing to acknowledge our truths, if we are willing to do the work.

In his conclusion of *The Wounded Healer*, Henri Nouwen shares that we don't need to live a life like Christ; that was His story. The secret is "to live your life as authentically as Christ lived his." It was a similar message that the Monsignor had given my Father when he left the seminary: "There are many ways to serve God." The answer is to live your own life authentically.

The very people we live among are in great need—physically, financially, emotionally, spiritually—and we can make a difference in the world wherever we are. I came to believe that I was where I was because this was where I was supposed to be. It didn't mean that I had to stay here forever. I just had to be present wherever I was.

The search for truth begins where you are.

I was born into this moment.

Postscript

IF THERE IS AN AFTERLIFE, then I believe that the one thing we, as humans, can all do to best prepare ourselves is to speak and live the truth.

I have had few regrets in life; however, earlier in this book, I did document the strongest of them. It was during my mother's final days in this world, and she had become much more open and vulnerable. I confessed how I had wished that I could have found the courage to be as equally open, to have shared more of my personal spiritual beliefs and experiences with her. I believe that it might have helped make her physical transition from this world much easier.

In the summer of 2017, I had a strong meditation where I re-experienced the regret I carried, and I wrote about it that evening in my journal.

The following day I found a sense of peace from reading of Dr. Mario Martinez's perspective on regrets. The timing was perfect. In *The Mindbody Self*, Martinez writes of how our lamentations serve little positive regard and are little more than disempowering thoughts, while the opposite, "Reclaiming what can be done," is in fact empowering. These empowering actions can be the literal means of "rescuing love from the dread," a means of filling the void.

I may not have shared my beliefs and experiences with my dying mother; I may have lost a beautiful opportunity. But the truth is I couldn't do things differently at that stage in my spiritual development. This was simply how my life played itself out. But I could and would share now. All is not lost. It never was. This book was my empowering action. I trusted that this book might be the means of rescuing love from a lost opportunity.

That was the final spiritual truth: to live a life without regret. To never have to ask, *Was it worth it?*

Acknowledgements

PERPHAPS THE GREATEST BEAUTY of writing a book on spirituality is that while you reflect on spiritual matters, you chance to gain a greater appreciation for what matters most in the worldly domain: family, friends, and animals.

A book of this nature could never be written in isolation. An author of my nature could never publish in isolation.

Thanks to my good friends Alan Edwards, Christine Gordon Manley, and the late Glen Edison for encouraging me to share my story. To my readers, Alan Edwards and Barbara McDowall, thank you for your insights, guidance, and friendship. To Terrilee Bulger, publisher and owner of Acorn Press: thank you for taking a chance on me, much appreciated. And a special thank you to my editor, Penelope Jackson, who reminded me that in writing, like life, intentions alone are never enough, and who was consistently mindful of my future readers.

Thanks to the co-authors of this journey called life: my brother, Hayden Smith; my maternal aunts Gracie, Mary Alice, and my Godmother Stella; and my children Carlye Mae, Dennis, and Riley, and their beautiful children. And sometimes you simply need that person who never wavers in their belief in you—thank you, cousin Michele.

Most of all, I thank Cheryl Thomson.